WITHDRAWN

Our Children, Our Friends

Our Children, Our Friends

Sheryl J. Andrews

THOMAS NELSON INC., PUBLISHERS
Nashville • New York

© 1977 by Sheryl J. Andrews

All rights reserved under International and Pan-American Conventions. Published in Nashville, Tennessee, by Thomas Nelson Inc., Publishers and simultaneously in Don Mills, Ontario, by Thomas Nelson & Sons (Canada) Limited.
Manufactured in the United States of America.

Library of Congress Cataloging in Publication Data

Andrews, Sheryl J
    Our children, our friends.

  1. Children—Management.   2. Family—Religious life.   3. Discipline of children.   4. Play. 5. Children in collective settlements.   I.   Title.
Hq769.A576   1977   649.'1   77–23513
ISBN 0–8407–5627–5

Table of Contents

Introduction		15
I	**LIVING TOGETHER**	**17**
	Who's in Charge Here?	19
	This Way, Please	27
	We Praise Thee, O God	31
	Get Yourself Together	42
	A Quiet Time	47
II	**CHILD'S PLAY: A TO Z**	**49**
	Art	51
	Books	57
	Cooking	60
	Large-Muscle Activities	63
	Music	66
	Rainy-Day Excursions	68
	Small-Muscle Activities	73
	Sunny-Day Excursions	76
	Traveling	81
	Waterplay	84
	Woodworking	87

III   LEARNING ABOUT EMOTIONS 89
       Male and Female Created He Them 91
       Blessed Are the Dead Who Die in the Lord 101
       A Heritage of the Lord: Handle with Care 107
       Bear Ye One Another's Burdens:
          Alternatives for Dealing with "School Phobia" 114
       Speaking the Truth to One Another in Love ... 119

IV   LOVE HOPES ALL THINGS 127
       Behaviors You Can Do Without 129
       The Supermom Myth 139
       Practical Results 144
       Train Up a Child in the Way 152

Acknowledgments

I am grateful to the family—George, Hal, Julie, Kelly, Booth, Shirley, Jay, Earline, Craig, Linda, and Karen, who all participated in the preparation of this manuscript, and who tenderly encouraged me every day; to Mozelle Core, who read the first draft and made many helpful suggestions; to my big brothers in the Lord, Don Finto, John Acuff, and Al Jaynes (who is also my big brother in the flesh), who read the manuscript for spiritual soundness and factual purity; and to Becky Porter who helped edit the work while she was supposed to be on vacation.

Exposure to the trophy-wielding baron
Without the indwelling Creator,
Reduces sophisticated world populations to
Vicious, salivating predators.
Still we continue to offer
Our children as living sacrifices
On the altars our God despises.

            Shirley Sheffield

For
the glory of God
to all parents
who really care.

Our Children, Our Friends

Introduction

This book is about a dozen people living as an extended family, bound together by the love of Jesus. George, the father, is a doctor by training and a patriarch by nature, a wise and gentle man who lives a life worthy of respect. I've had the good fortune to be married to him for twelve years. I am a teacher by training and a matriarch by nature. I am probably one of the few matriarchs married to a patriarch.

Our children are Hal, who is eight, and Julie, who was born a year later to the day. Kelly is five and a half and Booth just turned three.

Shirley came to live with us in 1969 when she was a senior in college. The children view her sometimes as a big sister and sometimes as their best friend. I see her as a gift from God.

Earline and Jay Kendall and their son Craig, who is thirteen, became family in 1972. I was serving on the board of a day-care center in the inner city. Earline was the director. As we worked together we realized we shared similar needs and values, and our two family units gradually became one.

In 1973 we all began spending weekends on a farm George and I owned which had formerly been used for a drug rehabilitation program. The Kendalls took over the mobile home on the property, and we took up residence in the house.

From 1973 through the spring of 1975, Earline and Shirley served in succession as directors of a day-care center known as Children's Center, Inc. During the 1973-74 school year the Center also served as an alternative school for older children, particularly Hal and Craig. Karen worked at the Center—as staff when there was money to pay her and as a volunteer when there wasn't. She and Linda, who is also a teacher, lived with us part of the time, and they have become family.

There are others who play supportive roles to the family by celebrating life with us when they can: Kip and Marilyn, Randy and Sarah, Robert, Liz, Martha, Susan, Becky, Jerry, Janice, Chris, Marie, and John. Leavy has a special place because he lived for a long time on very little money just because he believed in the idea.

This is the story of how we as an extended family cooperate in rearing the children. In the first section of the book I will describe the framework within which we operate as an extended family, and will expound our basic philosophy of child-rearing.

The second section focuses on children's play and describes in detail some of the activities we offer for the development of the whole child.

Section three discusses how we deal with some areas of high emotional impact: illness, death, school, sex, and honesty.

Section four points out ways to avoid undesirable behavior; it shares some practical results we have observed in the children; it dispells the Supermom myth; it offers suggestions and encouragement for implementing a program of structured growth.

I
LIVING TOGETHER

Who's In Charge Here?

We are not your average American medical family. George is a country club dropout. I don't belong to the garden club. Hal isn't in Little League and Julie hasn't joined the Brownie Scouts. God is number one at our house and Jesus Christ is revered as Savior and Lord.

We live two places all the time. When George is working, we live in a three-bedroom apartment in the suburbs of Nashville. Days off, we live in a large old farmhouse in Cumberland Furnace, Tennessee.

Because we have two residences, and since George delivers babies, there is no such thing as a schedule in our family. Some mornings we get up at the farm, drive to the hospital in town, and eat breakfast while Daddy makes rounds. Other mornings we get up in town and stop for a doughnut on the way to the farm. The children sleep equally well in their beds, in the car, or on the floor.

This constant upheaval does not disturb me. The children are growing into a world where changes are taking place with increasing momentum. Social institutions which formerly demanded respect have become corrupt or non-functioning. My philosophy is that the most important tools I can give my children are a faith in a living God, a respect for authority, an ability to share honestly with other people, and the flexibility to adapt to a changing world.

In order to transfer these skills and attitudes to the children we must operate within certain guidelines. The most important of the guidelines we follow is God's order for the family. Throughout the

Old Testament, God's promises were given to a man and his children and his children's children. The condition for receiving a blessing was obedience to God's order as set forth in His Word. Therefore, the first thing we establish at our house is who is the boss.

Daddy is the boss. He did not get to be the boss because he knows more about children than the rest of us do. He isn't the boss because he lords his sex or position over us. He is the boss because God says so. The truth is, he participates very little in formulating the way we train and discipline the children. He does support and reinforce what the rest of us do. When he disagrees with some decision we have made, we discuss it away from the children and change it to suit him.

If Daddy isn't home, Shirley or I am the boss. I learned a long time ago to trust that Shirley has a special understanding of children. Therefore, she is usually considered the last word if George isn't there. The children know I have ultimate authority if I choose to exercise it, but even if I disagree with what she does, we work it out between us when the children aren't there.

Earline, Jay, Karen, Linda, and even Craig offer suggestions about the training of the children. Some people marvel that George and I share the care and molding of our children so easily. Because we committed each child to God as he was born, we don't feel we have exclusive ownership. God gave them to us, we gave them back, and we trust Him for the wisdom and resources to train them for His service. Often He uses another family member to do His work and we can only be thankful. As a result, the children are products of multiple parenting.

We never consider adding an adult to the family unless he or she is responsible enough to parent and willing to treat each child with respect, gentleness, and love. Only those who believe in a personal and infinite God are allowed to relate to the children as a parent.

Beyond this, we have a wide spectrum of philosophies and life-styles in the family. Our combined educational experiences range from prep school to prison. The reason we are able to work together with a unified front is because our source of authority is the same and our goal is the same.

Whenever a change is made in the way we have been handling the children, we communicate this to each other. If a child needs to be

WHO'S IN CHARGE HERE?

disciplined, the person who initiated the action is responsible for following through. The rest of us offer support by being consistent with the child.

If an offender is sent to bed early, the one who sent him goes to the room after a few minutes and explains fully why discipline occurred. He tucks the child in with a kiss and the episode is finished. He does not feel remorseful and let the child get up. No one else goes to rescue the child, although several of us might stop by for a goodnight kiss.

If we are dealing with a very young child and he yells, we shut the door. We announce, as the door is closing, that we will open the door when the noise stops. Our older children don't yell. If the child is a toddler and he gets up, we put him back in bed and tell him not to get up again. If he gets up again, we put him in bed a little more forcefully. Once a course of action is initiated, we give it our full attention until the child does what we intended for him to do. We don't stay and listen to whining, nor do we change our minds about the discipline.

Often, when a child is being disciplined, he gets really angry. It is okay to be angry at our house. It is even all right to say so. One of the first complete sentences Booth said was, "You hurt my feelings." However, it is not acceptable for a child's anger to disrupt the entire household. Anyone who wants to be angry is asked to do so in his room with the door closed. As soon as he has himself together, he may rejoin the group.

We think it is important that each child learn to respect and obey appropriate authority. Once he accepts the chain of command, he is free from having to spend so much time finding out where the lines are drawn. He understands clearly what he is expected to do and to whom he answers. He also knows what to expect from us.

Making sure the child knows what to expect is an important part of our discipline. We call it "preventive discipline." One of our responsibilities is to explain what kind of behavior we expect as each task or outing begins. Whenever we introduce any new experience to the children, we discuss everything that is involved—what we are going to do, where, who else is doing it, how people usually act or react when they are doing it, and finally, what the acceptable behavior is.

This gives the child a standard to follow which prevents many problems. If a child strays from the prescribed course, a quiet reminder will frequently help check his behavior.

I did not invent preventive discipline all by myself. However, after having lived with the results for eight years, I would do it this way even if no one else in the family did. My children are not tied up in knots. They respond happily to new people and new situations. They are curious and feel free to explore. They are courteous and genuinely interested in each other.

While we are establishing authority, we also work on communication. I view children as little people. Big people need communication and companionship; little people require the same thing. Since their earliest efforts to communicate with me, I have tried to help them find the words to say what they really mean. In order to do this, I really have to listen to each child's tone and his body movements. If I don't, I might project what *I* feel instead of helping him uncover what *he* feels.

Sometimes I get preoccupied with what I'm doing, and I don't listen at all. Shirley might say, "Kelly called you four times and you haven't heard her yet." There are two reasons why I believe it is important for me to answer the children the first time they speak to me. First, it suggests I think what they say is important, which is true. Second, I expect them to respond to me the first time I speak to them, and it is only considerate of me to give them the same respect.

The children do communicate well, sometimes to the point of embarrassing the adults. We don't coach them, even though absolute truth is sometimes a monster in public. Anyone who talks with them gets the unedited version! Fortunately, they are very conscious of other people's feelings, and try not to freak them out.

A bonus that has come with the extra effort toward saying what one feels is that my children seldom argue with each other. All mothers of four know this is news worthy of headlines. If one of the girls comes in and says, "Hal did such and such to me," then I say, "Tell Hal," or "Did you tell him you don't like it?" They work out their own problems among themselves, and I don't even listen if I can help it. In fact, if I do hear it, I ask them to close the door.

There are, of course, exceptional situations. Sometimes one child doesn't understand what another child is trying to say. In that case, I try to restate what was said. This cuts down on the frustration of not knowing how to respond. Occasionally, one of the children will begin to irritate the others. They relate so well most of the time that it is easy to see who the culprit is. This means one of three things to me. The child is either very tired, getting sick, or he needs some special attention away from the others.

I deal with the problem by first asking the child to go to his room. After he has had a few minutes to settle down, I go in and chat with him about the day. This gives him a chance to reveal anything he needs to say. If no big problem falls out or he doesn't evidence symptoms which tip me off that he isn't well, I leave him in the room to rest. He nearly always falls asleep.

One day recently, after a time of vigorous activity, Hal was being really fussy. He usually doesn't act this way, so I just watched him and talked with him for a few minutes. I suggested a nap, and he sullenly said if he did go to sleep, he didn't want me to awaken him. I didn't, and he slept from three-thirty in the afternoon until eleven that night. After a sandwich and a cup of hot chocolate, he read until two in the morning and then slept until eight-thirty. When he awakened, his disposition had improved considerably.

Touching is another form of communication we teach the children to use. Doctors are taught to touch the patient because that makes the person feel he has the doctor's undivided attention. It is a way to say, "You are important," or "I'm listening to you."

There is, however, a difference between touching to communicate and petting a child. An example of petting is when an adult sees a cute child, feels benevolent toward him, and then uses the child as a love object by patting him on the head. This often violates the child's privacy and lowers his self-esteem.

Desirable communication by touching can occur when a child comes to you to say something and by his behavior indicates that he wants to sit on your lap or lean against you. Last night Hal asked me to rock him before he went to bed. Then each of the girls lined up for a turn. I didn't tell him he was too old to be rocked, because he was saying, "If you'd hold me for a few minutes, I'd really feel

Last night Hal asked me to rock him before he went to bed. Then each of the girls lined up for a turn

loved." Even at my age I love to be held, and I thought he made a valid request.

The family focus on gut-level communication and respect for authority ties in directly to how we share with them our faith in God. In helping the children search for a language that expresses what they feel, we have given them a tool for prayer. The heart of a little child is pure, and an answered prayer of a pure heart is a blessing.

Often, as adults, our prayers are not pure because we either don't know our inner selves well enough to say what we feel or we fear peer disapproval if we tell it like it is. Consequently, the answers we get are at best ambiguous, and at worst a downright curse. I know this is true because for years I prayed impure prayers. They were impure because often my mouth was saying what I thought it ought to, but my heart contradicted those words. We can't trick God; He hears and answers the prayer of our inner selves, our hearts.

Most of my life I have been in rebellion to authority. As a child I was subtle, as an adolescent I was sneaky, but as an adult I was flagrant in my disdain for authority. The result of this rebellion was years of wasted emotional and physical energy and legions of migraine headaches. Even though I was constantly uptight, I did not easily yield my right to challenge any philosophy which did not harmonize with my own.

I was finally beaten into submission by a series of circumstances which left me devoid of any self-esteem or even the physical energy to try to put the pieces back together. Once I understood God has a chain of command through which He bestows blessings, and that my proper place in the chain was under the headship of George, my life was transformed. My headaches became less frequent. I no longer believed I had to right all social injustice. My emotional and physical energies were free to be used in loving, creative outlets.

We teach the children their place in the chain of authority is under the parents. Because we too are under authority, George under Christ and me under George, we do not see this as a position of subservience. As the children obey me they learn to trust me. By experience they have learned I want them to live joyful, peaceful lives. They know they can trust me to supply physical necessities, emotional security, intellectual stimulation, social interaction, and spiritual intercession.

As I relate to God, my biggest hurdle has been learning to trust Him completely with my life. Often I have refused to obey Him because I am not sure He will let me have what I want. As I have learned to obey, I find I am right. Often He doesn't give me what I want. He gives me what I need, which always turns out to be a much larger blessing than what I asked for.

The children have learned to obey me, and they have found I can be trusted with their lives. As I have learned to obey God, I have learned to trust Him with mine. The children know I trust God the Father to supply my daily bread in the same way they trust me to supply their needs. Because we are secure in a Father God, our home is a haven of joy and peace. Hal, Julie, Kelly, and Booth have become individuals who really are as special as I felt they were the first time I ever held them.

Children who are conditioned to obey a higher authority are free to live peaceful lives. Those who are respected as individuals unfolding according to the design God placed within them are a joy to live with. They are a blessing to be near. That is why our children are our friends.

This Way, Please...

I was just sitting here watching Booth play in the rice. She has a cold, so we have cut out the waterplay for a few days. Before her she has two pans—a large cake pan and a cookie sheet. In the cake pan are measuring cups and spoons, a funnel, a large metal spoon, a baking powder can, and a piece of styrofoam the jelly jars came in. She dips the cup into the rice and pours it through the funnel into the can. When the can is full, she pours a neat pile on the cookie sheet. Then she dips back into the cake pan for more rice until the task is complete.

She has been pouring, measuring, feeling, and weighing the rice for almost an hour. She seems to be working almost feverishly, as if she were laying bricks and the building had to be finished by sundown. I've observed that the children are always serious about their tasks. It doesn't matter if they are finger-painting or helping with breakfast; they approach all work with a sense of wanting to do a thorough job.

We try to introduce each new task the same way we would like to be introduced to a new job. We explain or demonstrate the purpose of the task; we outline the boundaries within which the work should be done; we discuss the tools or equipment we will be using; we go over any safety procedures; and we tell the child what his responsibilities are for cleaning up after the job is done.

When Booth wants to play with the rice, she goes to the kitchen table. She knows the defined area of play. If she were to try to take a cup of rice to her bedroom, she would be reminded, "We play with rice at the table." If she tried to leave the table with the rice in tow again, her turn would be over! She has played with kitchen utensils since she could sit, so it isn't really necessary to show her how to use them. Shirley did suggest one idea by holding the funnel over a depression in the styrofoam. Booth was delighted and proceeded to fill all twelve holes with rice.

The first time she ever did this task, we told her to put all the utensils back in the cake pan when she was through. As far as she is concerned, this is part of the process, and she does it easily.

Although it sounds as if Booth has had to embrace a number of rules in order to play in the rice, she hasn't. She has been trained to play within a structure. There is an important difference between structure and rules. Structure defines the activity before it begins: where it will take place, what the purpose is, what materials are to be used, and what the child's responsibilities are. Structure is a positive approach because it eliminates bad choices and facilitates acceptable ones.

Rules, on the other hand, are usually negative. "We eat only at the table," is a positive presentation. "You get out of the living room with that cookie," is the negative counterpart. Rules usually result when the person in charge does not explain in the beginning what is desirable behavior.

Hal and Julie were babies when Shirley first came to live with us. At that time I was anxiously looking for ways to train them to be obedient without having to always say no. It seems like I was married before my father ever gave me a positive response the first time I asked permission of him to do anything. By the time I was sixteen I knew how many days ahead of time to ask to do something before he would change his mind and say yes.

The search for an atmosphere of positive order led me to a book about setting up Montessori tasks in the home. I began to experiment with some of the ideas and could see they facilitate what I wanted for the children—ordered play without a lot of restrictions. I always seemed to run out of suggested activities before the children ran out of energy.

While I was struggling with copying the suggestions in the Montessori book, Shirley was making great progress toward understanding the whole process of structure in raising children. She began to create play activities in many areas, and her experiments were obviously successful. However, it was several years before either of us could verbalize that the reason our children moved so easily through the day was that every activity was structured.

Even when tasks are structured toward success, problems sometimes occur. When a child refuses to cooperate with the plan, an attentive parent can guide the child into a successful experience anyway if he is willing to be as stubborn as the child.

Earlier this year, we had pinto beans set up in a task similar to the rice task. One day Booth played with it for a long time, and as she grew tired she poured the beans on the floor. I calmly told her to pick them up. She decided to see if I meant it. (She must have thought she was the first kid who ever tried this. Was she ever wrong! Every two-year-old I had ever dealt with had tried the same thing, and by the time she got here she was dealing with a pro.)

I don't remember how long she sat on the floor before she finally picked the beans up. The other kids went on a picnic and came back, the adults ate and straightened up, and she was still there. I didn't offer to feed her. When she asked to go on the picnic, she was told she could go as soon as she picked up the beans. Several adults and some of the children came through the kitchen and encouraged her to finish so she could do something else. Everyone acted as though they thought it was her job.

Eventually, she thought it over and decided maybe it was part of her responsibility. As she began to clean up, she also began to cry. This was the point at which she yielded her will to mine, and she was embarrassed and angry that she had lost. When she neared the end, I helped her and thanked her for completing the task. As soon as the beans were all in the pan, I picked her up and hugged her, fixed her a nice lunch, and tucked her in for a nap.

All rebellion is dealt with in a similar manner at our house. Because problems are communicated, they aren't allowed to grow. Since we explain before each activity what is acceptable behavior, it is fairly easy to identify where someone has missed the mark.

If a child does something wrong, we don't immediately decide he did it on purpose. When he is working at a new task, we go over the guidelines two or three times very carefully. Only when he has shown by previous performance that he understands what is expected do we initiate discipline if he disobeys.

Close supervision, especially of a young child, serves two purposes. It gives opportunity to adjust any accidental wrong performance of the task before it becomes a bad habit, and it allows for nipping deliberate misconduct in the bud.

The other day one of Julie's teachers told her she was a pleasure to be around. Julie replied, "That's because I've been trained." Even now Julie knows training is a blessing. Whenever someone places a new task before her, she knows approximately what questions to ask in order to gain information to do the job properly. Even if the person who presents the task does not outline the steps to follow, Julie can probe for directions. Because she has been trained from birth, she is equipped to share life experiences with both siblings and adults.

Our children are held in high esteem. They are sought as companions and their opinions are respected. Through early and intensive training, they have been given tools enabling them to participate with the adults in a celebration of life before the Lord.

We Praise Thee, O God

The theme of this book and of our lives is how we celebrate life before the Lord. This celebration is not something we just thought up one day. It is not the same as deciding to have a party and inviting guests. Neither is it the same as the traditional observances of special days.

In our family, the celebration of life before the Lord is a spontaneous outpouring of joy among a community of people who share similar values. The celebration often happens because we have come together to recognize a special event or a certain day, but the creative force behind the joy we share is God Himself.

It is because of our mutual allegiance to Jesus as Lord that such a diverse group is together in the first place. Since we serve a God who demands we love Him first and our fellow man second, each of us is bound to the other in a unique way. My daily goal is to grow toward fulfilling God's commands to love, obey, serve, and praise Him. I share that goal with each family member.

Any time we gather as a family, we have so many personal victories to share that the air is almost electric. If we are together because it is a holiday, or a birthday, or for some other event of special emphasis, we regularly witness an outpouring of music and creative praise before God.

To emphasize the difference between celebration and parties or rituals, I want to talk about the other functions first. Since early childhood I have enjoyed festive occasions. During my adolescence

I had the opportunity to attend many kinds of parties: banquets, house parties, teas, showers, and slumber parties. I approached each event with great anticipation and I entered into the merrymaking with all my energy.

After George and I married, I missed all these happy occasions, and so set about having parties to try to re-create some of those jolly events. I never hosted a party I felt good about. It is hard to remember even once when I felt like my guests really had a good time. The party just did not measure up to my expectations.

I have learned that many people party in an attempt to fill the void caused by the absence of interaction within caring groups. In an attempt to find meaning and joy, and to participate in celebration, they substitute a counterfeit of community called "parties."

At the time, I decided that being a good hostess must require some special training I had not received, so I turned my attention from parties to the observance of traditional holidays and family rituals.

I remembered that a sociology professor had once pointed out the important role that ritual and tradition play in cementing a family together. My own experiences confirmed this. One of my fondest childhood memories of my father centers around a Christmas ritual. Every year, the second Sunday before Christmas, he and I went to buy the tree. We always bought a freshly cut cedar tree. He indulged me by letting me select the largest tree possible for the space we had.

When we got the tree home, we stood it in a bucket and scotched it with rocks. He would string the lights, and Mother and I added glass balls and tinsel. Whenever my brother or sister were in town, they too would come for the tree trimming. Mother usually baked a country ham on tree-trimming Sunday. For supper, we had ham on warm rolls and ambrosia. Then we cut the fruit cake that had been aging in the lard stand. That was always a happy day for me. I remember the smell of the tree as the cedar aroma filled the house. I can still taste the juice that oozed out of the ham as Mother pushed cloves into it in a diamond pattern. She has a clear, sweet voice and would bustle around the kitchen singing carols.

New Year's Eve was also a special time for my family. We always took the tree down and placed the decorations in the attic. Mother talked about New Year's resolutions and encouraged me to make

WE PRAISE THEE, O GOD

some of my own. She and I would stay up until midnight and toast the New Year in with a glass of orange juice. My fond memories of those special days made me want to go home for them, even after I married. If I couldn't, my heart was still there.

My attempts at having good parties had failed, but I was sure that with my attention to detail I could establish a series of rituals in our home which would create an atmosphere of celebration. At first, we observed holidays in much the same way they had been carried out by my mother. However, as we grew into an extended family living in two places, my efforts to do things the way they had always been done became more and more frustrated.

On Christmas Eve of 1974 my suspicion was confirmed that you can do something similarly, but you can't do anything again. That year, we were going to be at the farm with the extended family for Christmas Eve, but we had to be in town by seven the next morning because George went on duty at that time. We intended to share a festive meal together and then open presents. We had planned the menu days in advance and spent the entire day preparing the food. In the afternoon, we built a roaring fire in the fireplace and gathered around the pump organ to sing carols.

About the time I gave the "fifteen minutes until supper" call, the man who farms our land dropped in. I offered him some spiced tea and made sure he understood that we were about to eat. He said he was on his way home to share Christmas with his children. I was relieved, because he tends to talk on and on. Two hours later, he was still there, rocking and talking about soybeans. George and Jay felt they must not be rude to him because he does us a favor by sharecropping our land.

I was furious. We held dinner as long as we could, and finally the women and children ate a semi-cold Christmas dinner by candlelight. I swore off any observance of Christmas ever again. After calming down, I realized the ritual had become more important to me than the people. If that was my attitude, I shouldn't be trying to encourage these activities anyway.

When I emotionally and verbally gave up the control of family festivities, I began to think of those days as times for being especially thankful to God for His goodness and care. Gradually, the thanksgiving turned me toward daily praise. Several other family members verbalized that they, too, were moving toward daily praise of the Father.

Linda phrased it well when she said, "I have learned to celebrate alone, because my celebration is an outpouring of what God has done in me—the joy He has created. But in order to celebrate with another person, there must be a meeting of God's doings: shared values, beliefs, a sense of community."

We had functioned for several years as an extended family. We had worked side by side, eaten together, and folded each other's laundry. We agreed with each other about training our children. We shared a belief in God the Father and Jesus the Son.

However, until we moved first individually, and then corporately, into praise unto God, we did not have the sharing of fullness which is found in true community. We had kept traditions and observed rituals, but they did not have the joy or spontaneity of a true celebration. We had held parties in an attempt to manufacture a sense of community and joy, but these parties often ended in debauchery and a feeling of emptiness. When the theme of our coming together became thanksgiving to the Father, we began to experience the joy and fullness of pure celebration.

This does not mean we have thrown all rituals out the door. I still prefer cedar Christmas trees and like to decorate them the second Sunday before Christmas. But it does mean each event special enough to be remembered is celebrated with a uniqueness that makes it distinct from all other events. We have given up the legalism of tradition. In return, we have received the freedom of celebration.

On the tree-trimming Sundays of my childhood, there was a certain order in which we moved that day. We went to pick out the tree in the middle of the afternoon. Then Daddy strung the lights. Next, Mother and I added balls and tinsel. If it wasn't done in that order, it didn't feel right. In the freedom of celebration, we set a time and place to meet. What happens after that depends on how the Spirit moves us.

In our family we have begun to set aside Sunday as a day of rest. Many people have observed either Saturday or Sunday as a rest day for years, but this is new for us.

Since we usually have our largest number of people at the farm on Sundays, we formerly used that day to tackle large work projects such as haying or fencing. While it provided rest in the sense that it was a diversion from each person's daily routine, it didn't leave us much time to focus on worship. George and I decided about a year ago our priorities were wrong, and we set aside Sunday as a day to rest and worship God in creative praise.

Creative praise may be a hike in the woods, a ballgame with the children, quiet meditation at the creek, gathering flowers for the table, singing or playing music, painting a picture, or even taking a nap. It is any activity in which the heart is centered on God, the body is yielded in purity, and the praiser is in some way refreshed.

Each Sunday is different. One morning, George and I took the children to a place near the creek and cooked breakfast. The other adults joined us later and we ate together. We sat around the fire and each person thanked God aloud for one special blessing they were aware of.

Another weekend, we announced on Saturday we would spend Sunday in an attitude of creative worship and come together at the end of the day to join in praise. In the morning hours, each person sought their favorite place for meditation. I gathered up my Bible and flute and went to the spring. Shirley read at her drawing table; others walked to the creek. Then, as if we had been given a signal, we began looking for ways to serve each other. Linda picked a bouquet for every room in the house. She even made small ones and placed them beside the children's beds. We gathered outside at sunset to commune and sing together.

Some of our family feel really grateful to the Lord for some extra sleep, so frequently we have a mid-morning breakfast. We try to get the entire group around the table, but sometimes we have to let all the children sit at a smaller, adjoining table. After the dishes are washed, we gather under a tree or in front of the fire to praise the Lord together. We try to make sure each child has a lap to sit on. Then we share songs, Scriptures, and prayer, letting the children participate equally with the adults. Toward the end of our worship, we commune with bread and wine.

Often, these times together are when personal problems or family crises are discussed. Anyone who has an opinion is encouraged to share it. Sometimes we unite on a course of action right then; other times we agree to pray about it together. One day recently, when we were facing a financial crisis, George called any of us who felt led to fast, to do so together before the Lord. Hal and Craig joined the fast. I fed the little girls, one member of our family who has had ulcers, and one who was pregnant.

It turned out to be a truly edifying day. We were all more sensitive to the needs of each other, and to the land. We rode all over the farm on horses, worked on Christmas gifts, played the organ, gathered walnuts, and shared the Word. When we began cooking, Linda brought her guitar into the kitchen and it seemed as though the whole family gathered to sing. (They were also in there because the food smelled very good.) Breaking the fast together was a true celebration of thanksgiving to God.

One day this summer, twenty of us gathered to sow a newly built dike with fescue seed. Marie told George she wanted him to baptize her that day. Hal told me he wanted to be baptized too, and I told him to discuss it with his daddy. He and George talked it over and George was impressed that he understood the significance of baptism.

The dike ended at the creek and George baptized both of them there. The remainder of the day was spent in jubilation for the new beginnings.

Contrary to my glum reactions to Christmas a year ago, we did have Christmas this year. We observed it on a Sunday, almost two weeks before the twenty-fifth, so most of the family members could participate. Each person was told to bring one dish of their favorite food plus gifts for the stockings. We initiated the festivities on Saturday by planting fruit trees. This was a happy project because it was an affirmation of faith that this land would be used for God's purposes for many years.

Early Sunday morning I baked some cookies shaped in the form of a horn of plenty. This was my declaration to the family that the Lord had blessed us richly. After Shirley woke up, she and I went in search of just the right tree. We scouted the fields and woods until we found it, but we didn't cut it right then.

As we started breakfast, I asked Karen and Becky to hang the stockings. They hung one for each person or couple, and nailed up several extras with the name "Elisha" on them. Elisha is the term we use for an unexpected guest. We always cook for him, so we felt we should also hang a stocking for him.

WE PRAISE THEE, O GOD

We already had one Elisha there that morning. Steve, a new Jewish Christian, had been invited to come along for the weekend, and when he saw the stockings he exclaimed it looked like Christmas for a centipede!

After a huge breakfast we gathered in the living room for worship. Linda shared Psalm 108 in the form of a song which had come to her. We sang songs of praise and thanksgiving, including "Jingle Bells." For Booth that is a praise song, so when she requested we include it in the worship, we did. Together, George and I served communion to the family. Even the adults recognize us loosely as Mom and Dad. As we offered the bread and wine to each person, we shared our joy that each one was a part of the family.

After communion, we hitched the hay wagon to the tractor and went to cut the tree. Some rode the wagon, others walked beside it, and Craig and Gaius rode behind on horses. As we rode along, the folks on the wagon sang carols to the treetops. Each person who needed a tree for his own dwelling selected one, and Jay and Shirley felled the farm tree.

During that time, Becky climbed up on a horse, slid off, and broke her wrist. She didn't mention being hurt until we got back to the house because she didn't intend to miss any of the activities. We wrapped her wrist in ice and George took her to the hospital. Jerry went along for moral support. Karen took charge of the kids, Earline moved into the kitchen, and Linda assumed responsibility for setting up and decorating the tree. Shirley looked after outside chores and ran errands.

We often divide areas of responsibility in this way. My job is usually to keep moving from one person to the other, consulting about problems and plugging in people who haven't been given a task. Obviously, this bearing of one another's burdens is a blessing. No one person has so much responsibility he is overwhelmed. Also, there is a feeling of being one part of a whole body. While each person realizes his contribution is needed, he doesn't have to be solely responsible for the end result.

As supper began to happen we realized another of the wonderful ways in which we are fitted together as one body. Without having discussed the menu, we had a nutritionally balanced, festive meal.

Linda brought cranberry tea and whole wheat rolls, Jerry contrib-

After communion, we hitched the hay wagon to the tractor and went to cut the tree.

uted sacks of fruit, Sarah made a chicken casserole, and Becky had chosen a broccoli casserole. (Fortunately she had put her dish together on Saturday night, because she came from the hospital with her arm in a cast.)

From the farm kitchen, we added steak and fried corn. Someone remembered there were turnips in the garden and we cooked those after Shirley and Gaius cleaned them. Karen had made boiled custard and others brought brownies, dried fruits, and nuts for dessert.

When we gathered in a circle to praise God for the day, David, a new resident at the farm, prayed, "Hallelujah, we declare this a feast unto You, and we welcome You as the Guest of Honor." When we spread the food buffet style, it truly did look like a feast.

Throughout the day, each person had gone to the fireplace and stuffed small gifts into the stockings. After supper we gathered to explore them. Even Steve, who was observing Christmas for the first time, had gathered up sticks and string and fashioned small crosses which he tucked into the top of each one. We had pinned his name to the toe of an Elisha stocking early in the day, and it looked as if everyone had prepared for Elisha. George's stocking held fresh oysters, snack crackers, and currant jam. Others had avocados, books, smoked sausage, lollipops, scented soap, artichokes, and homemade candy and cookies. The children had added drawings, painted rocks, and seashells.

After each item had been examined and savored, some of the weekend family who would be out of state on Christmas Day began to distribute gifts. Jerry had gone through her parents' attic and selected a doll each for Julie and Booth. She had obviously taken loving care of these dolls as a child, and I was overwhelmed at her love in giving them to my girls. For Kelly, she had an antique child's phonograph with a package of extra needles inside. Not only Jerry, but also Chris, Becky, Diane, Marie, and Randy and Sarah gave handmade, home-grown, or long-cherished treasures.

Even the few gifts that had been purchased were of a special quality. Randy and Sarah brought two gallons of soy oil and a gallon of honey to the family. Every family member will partake of that gift before the year is over.

As the day ended we sat in front of the fire and shared hymns and carols. Steve borrowed Linda's guitar and blessed us by singing "Silent Night, Holy Night." We sang "Jingle Bells" again for Booth. As each person left, I wrapped for them slices of country ham we had grown and cured on the farm. Each received a small jar of the sorghum molasses the family had made in the fall, and there was enough fresh fruit for each person to take a sackful. Give thanks unto the Lord, for He is good! Only He could empower us for such a celebration.

There are probably many parents who desire the experience of praise and celebration for their children, but do not have access to community. I am under the conviction that individual lives, given over to the Lord, will eventually draw other people who desire the same experience. The result of this coming together may be an intentional community, such as the one we share, or an association with less intensity, such as a once-a-week support group.

Our extended family is a microcosm of the church we attend when we are in town. One of the shared values which brought us together was the recognition that the Bible classes offered for our children did not accurately reflect our philosophy of how children should be trained. We began to gather on Sunday nights for supper and discussion, long before we had access to the farm. The families who attended those meetings began to explore the idea of Christian community. Some dropped out because they didn't agree with our child-rearing practices; a few were not ready to accept community as a solution to the anxiety they felt.

The congregation we worship with when we are in town is rather unusual. It consists of a large group of middle-class families and college students who have chosen to minister to people in the inner city. In the neighborhood there are black families, foreign students, and older white people who grew up there and never moved away. Also in our fellowship are ex-convicts, converted homosexuals, reformed drug addicts, janitors, college professors, corporation presidents, and entertainers. Everyone comes as they are. When this group comes together, the only thing we have in common is the lordship of Jesus in our lives.

For my children to come as they are often means they wear shirts with three shades of paint on them. The white stockings may have grass stains or holes in the knees. They have clothes which look much better, and sometimes they choose to dress up, but we don't insist on it.

Every day we share with them some form of worship, praise, or thanksgiving to God. We believe worship is a minute-by-minute, day-by-day communication with the Father. We think it is walking with holy bodies before our Creator. Therefore we feel it would be inconsistent to teach the children God does not accept their adoration if they are not properly dressed.

Not all parents in our fellowship share this point of view. We can worship together because we have come to lift up Jesus, not to look at each other.

The Sundays we worship in town are also set aside as days of rest. We have never announced it publicly, but many people know our apartment is open to them if they seek fellowship. After worship we usually gather at a nearby restaurant as a group or go to the apartment and have a light lunch. The afternoon is spent playing ball or tennis or sailing or napping. We have very little room, but we still manage to serve supper to fifteen to twenty people Sunday night. I told a friend recently that we live in a heap more peacefully than most people live spread out.

It is a blessing to have the farm to go to, but the celebration which flows from community can spring forth in any physical setting. The parent who sets his heart to praise the Lord will find God provides joy for the occasion. His mercies are new every morning!

Get Yourself Together

One day when George was off work, we dropped in at Mother's around lunchtime. She offered to feed us and we accepted. She moved to the kitchen in a flurry to make bacon, lettuce, and tomato sandwiches. Booth followed her and was surprised to see her spreading newspapers around the stove. Booth asked, "Grandmother, what are you doing?" Mother replied, "I'm going to fry some bacon." Booth exclained, "On the floor?"

I grew up in a home where when it came time to spring clean, you couldn't find anything to do. My pet name for my mother is "Mrs. Clean." By the time I started to school my brother and sister were grown and gone so Mother did a super job of keeping the house together.

We were a lower-income family in our community, and I remember that the summer my mother began working I had only one set of play clothes. She came home every night and washed them out by hand so they would be clean. I was taught at an early age to make the bed when I got out of it and to wash the pans as I got supper ready. My own need for orderly surroundings was well developed by my mid-teens.

When George and I married, I started off in high gear keeping the apartment straight. I thought one of the ways you make a husband feel good is to keep his kingdom in order.

Soon after we married, George's parents came to visit us for the weekend. We lived in a basement apartment in a dirty city so the window sills were continually covered with soot. I usually dusted them twice a day, and I was so busy keeping the place picked up and dusted I didn't have a lot of time to sit down and visit.

Before the weekend was over my father-in-law talked gently with me and explained a couple of things. He reminded me I was married to a man who was going to be a doctor, and for the next several years of school and training and even in private practice, the amount of time he would be at home would be limited—consequently, particularly precious. He said it was more important for me to really communicate and share good times with George when he was home than to sweep the floor. I got the message.

Since I was also a student, as I began to try to put this advice into practice my house started to fall apart. We had purposely scheduled as many classes at the same time as we could, so I was rarely home when George wasn't. I began to feel really guilty about the apartment being messy, but George told me as long as there was a path to the table, the bathroom, and the bed, he didn't care what the rest of the house looked like.

Consequently I degenerated into a terrible housekeeper. Anytime my house is absolutely together, I am either expecting company, I have just spring cleaned, or I'm clearing out my head.

This may suggest we live in bedlam, but that isn't true. The physical order at our house is all internal. The spices are alphabetized on the rack; the butter is on the top left-hand shelf of the refrigerator; Julie's shirts are in the second drawer from the bottom on the right-hand side of the dresser, and I have memorized where every item in the medicine cabinet is supposed to be. I have compromised external order for internal order. I can find any item in our house in sixty seconds unless someone has moved it.

Since we constantly move back and forth from the apartment to the farm, I am satisfied with this arrangement. Just the sheer mechanics of living in two houses means we're always piling stuff by the door to take to the other home, but when it gets there it has a special place to go. I can walk around and over all kinds of obstacles as long as the cabinets, shelves, closets, and drawers are in order. When they get messed up, I really feel depressed and we have to shovel out.

The children understand my priorities for order. When they were toddlers, I began to teach them to put their shoes beside their bed when they took them off. When Shirley or I put their clean clothes up, we always put the socks, shirts, and pants in one certain place. We even had specified shelves for each toy. By the time they were eighteen months old we began to show them where to put their toys when they were through playing with them.

About once a week all the adults and all the children pitch in and pull the house together. The rest of the time the kids keep their rooms however they want them. It would be inconsistent for me to let the rest of the house go while expecting them to straighten their rooms. Two children live in each room. Each child has a bed, part of a dresser, a closet, some shelves, and one side of the room which is his or her domain. On clean-up days they are responsible for straightening their own areas. Booth has to stand on her bed to make it because it is wedged in on three sides. Even so, she does a really good job.

I think it is crucial for children to have defined spaces that are theirs. This develops a respect for privacy and other people's property. It gives them total control over a small area of their lives; how they arrange their space is strictly up to them. Hal once received a horse poster he was really proud of. He asked me if he could nail it to the wall over his bed. I told him it was his poster and his space and he could nail it to the floor if he wanted to.

They should also have their own toys and the right to decide whether or not to share them. I don't let one child use another child's personal property unless he first asks permission from the owner. If the owner isn't at home, he has to wait.

We also let each child decide what he wants to wear. When a child is a toddler we pick out two outfits and let him decide between them. As he gets older he is offered suggestions on which colors match well, what goes with checked pants or a striped shirt, and by the time he is five, we give him freedom of choice about what he wears.

I also let him go with me to buy the clothes. After he understands what type of clothes we are shopping for, he gets to pick which ones he wants. It is fairly easy to see the children are in control of their wardrobes. One day Julie wears pantyhose and a nice dress to school, and the next day she might select play clothes with patches on the knees.

Hal has always disliked dressing up. The only time I made him do it was for my parents' fiftieth wedding anniversary party. I explained

GET YOURSELF TOGETHER

that this time was special to them, and he didn't have a choice about dressing up. He did go to the store to select what he would wear.

We often go places where it is expected you will wear something other than jeans. If Hal doesn't want to comply, I just leave him with someone else. As he gets older and wants to do more things, he has taken the initiative to make sure there are some clothes in his wardrobe he can dress up in.

The children are also responsible for putting their dirty clothes in the right spot so they will be washed; I don't go through their rooms and gather the clothes. If they run out of socks they have to borrow a pair, wear a pair that doesn't match from the sock sack, or wear dirty ones. It is their problem about what they do, not mine. When a child runs out of something, he gets real busy getting all his dirty clothes to me. When children are allowed to live with the consequences of their negligence, they become more responsible.

When we first begin encouraging a toddler to pick up after himself, he joyfully cooperates. At this age, putting up is as much fun for him as taking out or playing with it. There comes a day, however, usually around the age of three, when the little person realizes cleaning up is a drag. He then sets out to beat the system.

Whenever the children are straightening their rooms and a child finishes his area, we let him move on to another activity he chooses to do. A child stays in his room until his space is clean.

The day Kelly realized cleaning was work, she put up a real resistance. Julie finished her side and came to breakfast. Kelly just sat there. I went in and admonished her to finish and pointed out a couple things that needed to be done. She just sat there. I closed the door and told her to come out when she was through. For three hours it was very quiet in there. Every thirty minutes I opened the door to make sure she was all right. She didn't yell or fuss; she just sat there. By this time it was ten-thirty Saturday morning. The other children had eaten long ago and were watching cartoons.

When she realized I really wasn't going to feed her or let her out until she did her work, she began to cry softly and started picking up. I appeared with praise for what she had done and encouragement to finish. I stayed with her the last few minutes and told her what a fine job she had done and how nice her room looked.

From that day on, Kelly could clean up faster, more thoroughly, and usually more joyfully than any of the other children. That morning when she yielded her will to mine was painful, but it was only one day. The benefits have been more than worth it.

Our family is comfortable with our kind of order. We realize not everyone is. My mother can hardly bear to look. If we know she is coming, we do our best to get the house straight enough for her to feel at ease. When we go to her house, we all try very hard to assure her we respect her cleanliness and will try to keep it that way. She has lots of glass knickknacks, pictures, plants, and lamps. My children are fascinated with them. They all have been given the word to keep their hands off them.

Soon after Hal was born, I suggested to Mother that she let the closet in the den be the children's domain. She agreed, and filled a cardboard box with dime-store toys; about once a year she adds new ones. When we go to her house the kids know they can go straight to that closet and drag out the toys. When we are ready to leave, they pick things up and shove the box back in. You can hardly tell we've been there.

I encourage Mother or anyone else whose home we are visiting in, to set their own limits for the children. Since we are guests, I believe both the hostess and the children are more comfortable if they communicate directly what is or is not acceptable behavior. If the expectations of the person we are visiting are too unreasonable, we don't go there very often.

A Quiet Time

For a while, I was the mother of four children five years of age and under. A friend once told me, "Two is one more than one and three is eighty more than two."

In this situation, survival becomes a prime concern. By the time Booth got here, Hal was just about finished with naps, and I had visions of that precious nap time slipping away. At this point, Shirley's genius invented "quiet time," a two-hour period in the middle of the afternoon when the children are isolated from the adults and from each other. I must confess that at first I thought this was created to serve my purposes instead of the children's, but my need for a break was so acute I didn't question it.

Shirley explained that today's children are confronted with so many stimuli that they need a time to sort out ideas themselves. We have been able to see the continuing value of a quiet time for the children in their development of self-discipline, creative expression, and advanced cognizance.

When the children first begin to resist a nap we set up activities for them to do during quiet time. We have several Fisher-Price toys with people, cars, and furniture which we keep on a shelf and offer as a choice during this period.

Sometimes Booth settles down with a couple of wooden puzzles and a *Sesame Street* magazine. Other times she will play with blocks for a long time on her bed. She usually falls asleep before the two hours have passed.

Kelly enjoys cassette tapes with read-along books, view-master pictures, puppets, or just a good coloring book with a whole box of crayons. Julie is the gift-giver at our house and is frequently drawing a picture or wrapping a gift she has made.

One day recently she spent two hours writing, cutting out, and taping to the wall the phrase "I love you." I didn't count how many she put up, but apparently she did because she asked me if I thought she had one for each person who visits us regularly.

Hal is an active person who would probably never choose to be still for two hours unless someone made him. I'm sure one of the reasons he reads so voraciously is because he has been forced to make some quiet choices.

By the time a child is five, he is responsible for his own quiet time activities. We help him gather materials and then he is on his own for the next two hours. If he runs out of activities, then it is his responsibility to plan better next time. The children are expected to stay where they began quiet time unless they get sleepy and want to nap. This frees me of having to worry about them, and I can nap too if I want.

The time immediately following this rest period is a time of focusing on the individual needs of each child. We hold each one in our laps while we put on shoes or braid hair. If it is going to be a while until supper, we offer a snack like fruit, nuts, popcorn, or hot chocolate. When there is time, we let each child select a game, book, or activity he wants to do and share it on a one-to-one basis with him.

II
CHILD'S PLAY: A TO Z

All learning moves along a continuum. Each activity a child undertakes contributes to his physical, intellectual, social, emotional, and spiritual growth. I have ordered the tasks in this section alphabetically, hoping that when read together, they will present suggestions and challenges for the growth of the whole child.

Art

Art can be done indoors or outdoors, in good or bad weather, alone or in a group. It can be a noisy or a quiet activity. Children are exposed to different colors and textures through art. They learn primary and secondary colors. Various surfaces are not only seen, but experienced.

Art activities develop responsibility in a young child. Anyone who wants to paint more than once or twice quickly learns to wash out brushes and not to leave the cans of powdered tempera in the rain. Since supplies are expensive, few families can offer continuous art exposure unless the children are taught to help care for the materials. Children also sense the pleasure of having the last word as they exercise control over the art medium. They decide what color and how much and when they are finished.

Sorting is a pre-reading skill all children must develop. Since Booth was eighteen months old we have given her the opportunity to sort art materials. She thought putting the scissors in one pile, the crayons in another, and the brushes in still another pile was a delightful game. She also had the satisfaction of seeing it is a real service to others.

She also began painting at this age. We would cover her with a large bib, stand her at a child-sized table, and give her a couple cans of paint and large brushes. In the minutes that followed she was captivated by the blending of colors and the motion. When she was through, we would tell her we were going to put her name on the picture and with the paint brush would write "Booth." We always put the child's name on his picture as he or she finishes.

Children move through a series of stages in developing eye-hand coordination. This coordination is a prerequisite for all written communication. Art allows for a natural progression of these stages, and our children usually make their earliest attempts to write letters as they paint.

Hal hounded us when he was two to teach him the names of the letters on his alphabet blocks. Kelly, on the other hand, never mentioned numbers or letters. One day when she was four I looked at the easel and realized her "picture" was the letter "K." Since she had seen her name written on every piece of art she had ever done, the "K" just flowed out.

We have a designated place in each dwelling where art supplies are kept. The linen closet next to the guest bathroom is the "art room" at the apartment. In it are newsprint, construction paper, colored tissue, velour paper, and paper for finger-painting. On one shelf are dry and liquid tempera, finger-paint, assorted felt-tip pens, colored pencils, crayons, all sizes of brushes, glue, large pencils, scissors, staples, tape, and string. There are also several inked stamp pads and rubber stamps with letters, numbers, and figures on them. We have stored stacks of newspapers to spread under art activities. At the farm we store art materials on a bookcase beside the dining table. Since the children often paint on wood or rocks out there, we have sets of acrylics, oils, and watercolors in addition to the powdered paints.

The adults in our family frequently participate in the art activities with the children. We paint or paste side by side. This gives us opportunities to express our preconceived products ourselves rather than trying to infringe on the children's expressions.

This summer, about a month before Hal, Julie, and Booth were to have a birthday, I asked Earline to show us how to make piñatas out of papier maché. We set a table under the apple tree and pitched in shredding newspapers. Then all four children and Shirley and I each worked on a creation.

I molded a snake over a long balloon, and Kelly made a crab over a mixing bowl. Shirley turned a plastic milk jug into a pig, and Julie plastered a rubber playground ball. Earline stood by to point out

The day of the birthday party Earline filled each piñata with dime-store toys and candies, and the children took turns being blindfolded and swinging a stick to open them.

places that needed to be reinforced. We dipped the strips in liquid starch and then layered them for an hour.

As the newspaper dried, the objects were taken off the molds. Then they were taped together, leaving an opening to put goodies in, and painted with tempera. The day of the birthday party Earline filled each piñata with dime-store toys and candies, and the children took turns being blindfolded and swinging a stick to open them. This activity added much to the atmosphere of celebration we enjoy sharing with the children.

The children do many collages at the farm. Shirley and I have a box where we place bottle tops, bits of ribbon, burned matches, pieces of toys which are broken or lost, and anything else small enough to glue on paper. Sometimes we gather wild flowers or seedpods. When we have a good assortment we spread newspaper, refill each child's glue bottle, and pass out construction paper or cardboard. My children will stay with this activity until the materials are used up.

On occasion we take them to the creek and let them gather stones. Our creek is full of small fossils and blue rocks, which are slag from an old iron furnace. When each child has a pocketful of stones, we help him select a piece of slate or other large rock to glue his stones on. We use rock collages for bookends, paperweights, doorstops, and knickknacks.

Many mothers shudder at the thought of letting a small child glue anything. One of Shirley's favorite art experiences for toddlers is letting them glue. She used to place four of them around a table at the Children's Center, pour the glue into tin pie plates, and give each child a brush to spread it with. Then she put an assortment of items in the center of the table for them to select and glue. Sometimes it was magazine pictures, cloth scraps, beans, packing material, or torn tissue paper. Once she used the letters and numerals from a worn-out lettering set. As each child grew tired of the activity she would wipe his hands and send him to a different area. Then another child had a turn.

I think one of the most exciting activities they ever did at the Center was plexiglas sculpture. Earline found a supplier who would donate scraps of plexiglass. Shirley placed a couple of lighted candles in the center of a table and let two children at a time hold the plexiglass in the flame until it melted, then blow it out and press the edge to another piece of plexiglass. This was an outside activity and only the two children whose turn it was were allowed near the table. They were constantly supervised, and not one ever got scorched.

Last year before Christmas, the Center children made plaster of Paris figures. Shirley bought two sets of molds, one a group of farm animals, the other a nativity scene. Since these children were a mixture of social classes, ethnic groups, and religions, no teacher mentioned making these for Christmas. Each child made three figures of his choice. Some of the older children whose families were observing Christmas tied the activity to that holiday. All the children were proud of the results, and after the figures had been displayed for a short time they took them home.

The Center staff did recognize Christmas by putting up a large Christmas tree. The children made all the decorations except the tinsel. They shaped, baked, and painted dozens of dough figures and added yards of paper chains. Since there were no lights on it, the tree remained a couple of weeks after Christmas and the kids continued to play with it. They rearranged the decorations at least a dozen times; there was no doubt it was their tree.

For the last two or three weeks Shirley has been making Christmas cards. Last weekend she cut several designs into pieces of potato and made prints with them. She showed me one picture Booth did of flowers and crosses. Shirley said Booth first painted onto the potato with a brush and then printed the design onto paper. She was using tempera mixed with glycerine and was printing on construction paper.

We have also done rubbings of fall leaves this week. While visiting a playground near the lake we picked up several leaves of different sizes and shapes. When we got home we spread newspaper, placed one or two leaves close together, and laid a piece of newsprint over them. Using the side of a crayon, we rubbed the newsprint until the details of the leaf began to show. Other items we have used for rubbings are carpet scraps, sandpaper letters, coins, and cardboard animals.

At the farm we have even done rubbings of tombstones in an old cemetery on the property. We tape a piece of butcher paper to the top of the stone and use dark colors against the white paper so the words will be sharper.

Another thing we sometimes do with broken crayons is paint with them. We let the children peel the paper and sort them by colors into the cups of a muffin tin. Then we melt them in a warm oven for about an hour. When the colors are liquid, we use brushes to paint onto small pieces of cloth.

One of the activities Leavy used to do with the four- and five-year-olds was body drawings. He would let each child lie down on a piece of butcher paper. Then he used a felt pen or large crayon to trace the outline of their bodies. The children would then color in their hair, eyes, socks, shoes, and clothing. This allowed the children to compare sizes, shapes, similarities and differences, and learn color discrimination such as light blue versus dark blue.

Sand casting was a favorite task of Shirley's and something the children always enjoyed. It can be done in a sand table if one is available; otherwise a large cake pan will work. Water is poured on the sand until it will hold an impression. The children can then use their hand or some blunt instrument to create a design or impression. Plaster of Paris is then poured into the relief and allowed to harden. When it is removed the sand is brushed away and the creation can be painted.

An alternative to plaster is paraffin. After the impression is made, a wick can be tied to a pencil and held in place while hot wax is poured into the mold. When the paraffin hardens it can be lifted from the sand, brushed off, and burned as a candle.

Books

Books are "in" at our house. The adults and children could build a substantial shelter out of our combined libraries. George's collection is medical; mine is farming, history, and travel; Shirley's is alternative lifestyles and novels; and all of us have a religious collection. Hal has a budding collection of horse and football stories and the girls have many Dr. Seuss, Brian Wildsmith, and Richard Scary books. Earline has a large professional library on early education; Linda also has a sizable collection.

Until three years ago, I had never spent the night on a working farm and never planted a garden. This year I helped plan, plant, cultivate, harvest, and preserve everything from asparagus to zucchini. The knowledge of how to do this came almost exclusively from books.

My need for new information is so acute that I regularly arise two hours before anyone else does at my house so I can read. This enthusiasm for reading seems to be contagious. Each child has a selection of books beside his or her bed so they can read when they wake up in the morning.

Since school opened, Hal has checked out two library books every day. If he hasn't read them by the time school is over, he finishes them as soon as he gets home. Julie has begun to devour books in the same manner. As soon as Booth could sit alone, she had a book in her bed.

We often read aloud to the children, especially at bedtime. Last winter I read *Charlotte's Web* aloud one chapter at a time at bedtime; before we had finished the book, the children were offering to go to bed early so we could read.

There is no emphasis on reading as a science. None of us has ever sat down to teach one of the children to read. Since the children are eager to take their place in the adult world, and since books are such an obvious part of that world, they usually begin to pester us to help them with words around the age of five. We do reinforce them positively for reading. Often at bedtime a child will ask if he can read before he goes to sleep. The answer is always yes. Since we are pretty rigid about getting to bed on time, being allowed to read late is a reward.

The children's exposure to books is strengthened because of the contributions from the extended family. Earline is a walking resource on good children's literature. She regularly makes trips to the library where she selects several books for each child. She comes in carrying a box of books and the children descend on her. If we would let them, they would read in one day every book she brought.

Shirley is really good about sitting down with the children piled all over her and reading a story. She really enjoys most of the stories, and the children catch her enthusiasm. One of her favorite books is Maurice Sendak's *Where the Wild Things Are*. Hal wore out two copies of that one in a year's time.

The public libraries in Nashville have a story hour for preschoolers once a week, and we usually take Kelly and Booth. Recently they showed a film called *Caterpillar* which was one of the cleverest movies I have ever seen. They also have a storybook princess who dresses in costume and tells the children stories.

On Friday night at the main library there is a puppet show. Tom Tichenor is the genius who stages these shows. He is world famous for the Broadway shows he has done and for his children's shows. He designed a story room there with a fireplace, a hooked rug, and benches for the mamas. Built into the wall are display cases with exhibits he changes with the seasons. One of my favorite displays is the bear house—a doll-house type structure furnished for and inhabited by a family of storybook bears.

In addition to a house full of books, and regular visits to the library, we use a variety of audio-visual supplements to encourage an interest in reading. We own an eight-millimeter projector and the library has cartoons we sometimes check out and show. These are silent movies, but the children like them as well as films with sound. This is a good activity for children on a bad day. We just pop some corn and play like we're at the movies.

We have a set of childrens' stories on cassette tapes with read-along books. Everyone over age five is allowed to work the tape player, and Kelly especially enjoys these stories. One Sunday afternoon not long ago the children and I listened to the story of Cinderella. Then each of us selected a puppet and acted out the story. I chose a pig to be the stepmother and Kelly selected an alligator to be the prince. I was the narrator and the children sometimes read and sometimes ad-libbed their lines.

We take many photographs and slides, and one of our favorite language development activities is to show the slides and let the children tell about them. Every time I get a new set of pictures back from the printer, a thirty-minute discussion ensues on what we were doing the day the pictures were taken.

There is a television at our house, but I think most of what comes out of it is destructive. The exceptions are the children's shows on public television and selected shows on the networks. I regularly buy a *TV Guide* in order to edit what the children see.

We don't subscribe to popular magazines or newspapers for the same reason we don't watch television. I really believe children become what they think about most, and I don't intend to feed mine a regular diet of violence and rebellion. We do subscribe to several children's magazines such as *Highlights*, *Sesame Street*, and *Ranger Rick*. *Ranger Rick* is printed by the National Wildlife Federation and is full of color nature photographs. Hal confided that the subscription renewal to it which Linda gave him was his favorite birthday present.

Cooking

Karen made an applesauce cake with the girls today. It was one of those yummy kinds with lots of spices, nuts, and dried fruits. Since Julie is the oldest she got to measure the applesauce. Kelly measured raisins, and Booth filled a measuring cup with nuts. One child greased the pan, one sifted dry ingredients, and another broke the eggs. Everyone got to stir. The cake was delicious and as soon as quiet time was over we served each child a large piece.

I used to be such a perfectionist that I couldn't stand to cook with the children. Happily, I've gotten over that. Now whenever one of the children signal me by their behavior they need a little extra time, I get them up to cook breakfast with me. They count out the pieces of bread, butter them, break the eggs, mix juice, lay the bacon strips on the pan, and set the table. Booth already knows you add milk and salt to eggs if you are going to scramble them.

Some mornings we make coffee cake, or pancakes, or apple fritters. Hal made a coffee cake by himself recently. I just stood by to find ingredients for him. One day we made yeast doughnuts, the kind that take nearly all day. We mixed them in the morning, and Hal and Julie helped knead them. During quiet time I made one bowl each of chocolate and vanilla glaze. When the kids got up, I fried and drained the dough, and each child dipped his any way he wanted to. Daddy had to work that night, and we were so stuffed with doughnuts that the kids voted to skip supper.

One morning this summer when the blackberries were ripe, we got

COOKING

the whole family up early and went pickin'. Each child, including Booth, had a small container, and as we spotted thick growths of berries we would show them where to pick. We picked about two hours. Kelly dropped her berries twice and everyone got a few scratches, but eventually we gathered a couple gallons of fruit.

When we got home each child from Booth to Craig went through the steps of making jam: washing and sorting, mashing, measuring with sugar, stirring, filling the jars, and pouring the paraffin. Craig commented he had no idea so much work went into a jar of jam. Each child picked out a private jar of jam and stashed it away. I have never asked what they did with them. They may have given them away or eaten them or kept them.

Booth really enjoyed this activity and she sat on a stool and mashed berries for over an hour. I gave her a cup to dip with and told her to add more when those were mashed. She got to decide when the berries were mashed enough and how many more to add, and she did fine.

I regularly turn the kitchen over to the kids, and they fix their own lunches. Craig is tall and can reach the bread and peanut butter. They love to pack a lunchbox and head for the creek for lunch. They know it is a privilege to use the kitchen, and they do a good job of cleaning up.

Some interesting creations have come out of kitchen privileges. Julie asked me one afternoon if she could make a cake if she cleaned the kitchen when she was through. I told her she could and went on with what I was doing. Sometime later she brought me her cake to admire. She had included all her favorite things like brown sugar, maraschino cherries, and marshmallows. In fact, that was the whole cake, but it was arranged very appealingly in a cake pan. She then began to offer everyone a piece and—bless Jay—he took a piece and even got a couple of bites down without making a face. (Jay became special to the family at that moment.) About that time Julie started eating it and quickly announced it wasn't quite right and told Jay he didn't have to eat it if he didn't like it.

Hal has created some recipes for candy. One day I was looking through the recipe drawer and found a piece of paper with Hal's printing on it. A little investigation revealed he had made up this conglomeration and written it down as he went.

Even if I'm making lunch, one of the children often helps me. I really prefer to work with them one at a time because I don't get distracted that way. They chop eggs and pickles on the cutting board, grate cheese, or spread mayonnaise on the bread. Setting the table is a great counting exercise, especially at our house where the number changes every meal. I never remember the napkins, but Booth does.

At the apartment the only dishes I have are my wedding crystal, china, and silver. We eat from them every meal, and not one piece has ever been broken. When we moved into the apartment all this finery had been stored in boxes, and I decided it was time to use it. I didn't expect to ever entertain anyone more important to me than my own family. The children always remove their own plates, glasses, and silverware from the table. Hal and Julie alternately clear the rest of the table and wipe it off. Booth and Kelly take turns brushing off the chairs.

Large-Muscle Activities

This afternoon all the kids played on two sets of old metal bedsprings out in the back yard. We have been drying sorghum seeds on them, and after the children cleaned the seeds off, we let them jump. I kept waiting to sew a finger back on, but the worst that happened was Booth's cowboy boot got stuck a couple of times. They jumped for almost two hours, making up games and stunts as they went.

Last summer our waterbed sprang a leak. George patched it first with bubble gum and then with a vinyl glue but we were both afraid to sleep on it, so we bought a new mattress and gave the old one to Shirley, who put it out in the yard. The children slept, jumped, and rolled on it for two or three months.

Other large-muscle builders which are handy to have around (and more available than bedsprings or waterbed mattresses) are plastic milk crates. They can be transformed into houses, pyramids, tables, stools, suitcases, shelves, or toy boxes. Booth likes to sit in one and pull another one over her head and hide. They really are marvelous inventions, and we have about a dozen which travel back and forth between our dwellings.

In Booth and Kelly's room at the farm there is a wooden climber. It is about five feet tall and has a ladder up each side and one across the top. Right now there is an old baby-bed mattress under it, but at other times we have put a beanbag underneath so the children could drop off safely to the floor. The older children are now able to make their

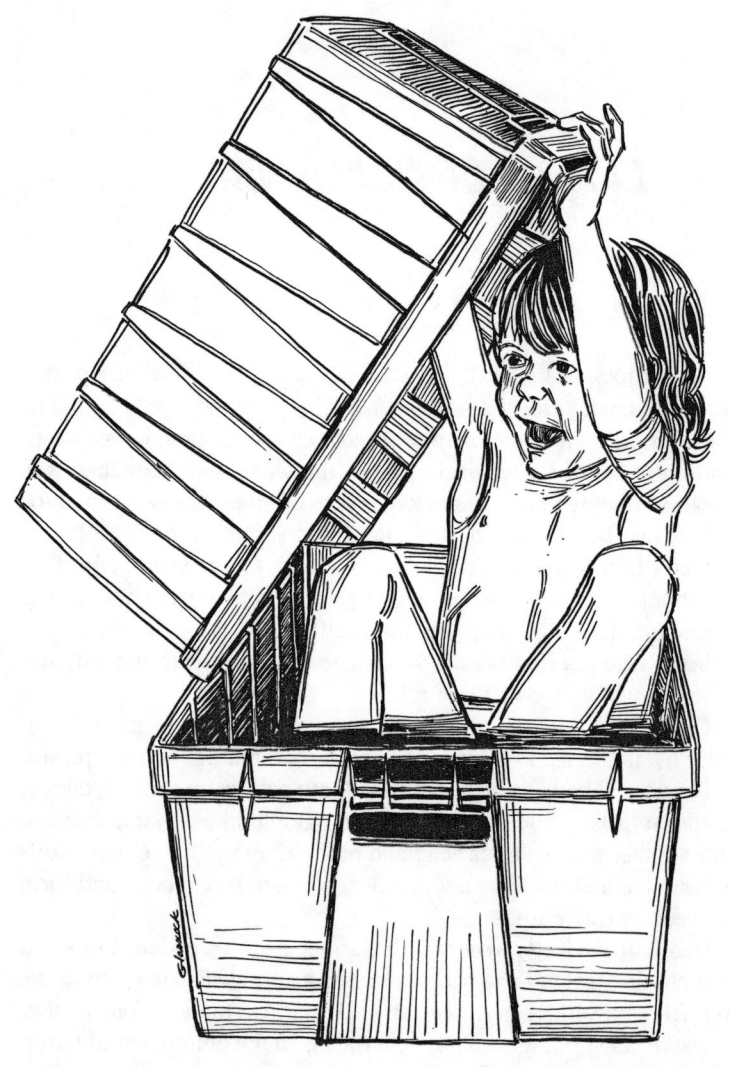

Booth likes to sit in one milk crate and pull another one over her head and hide.

LARGE-MUSCLE ACTIVITIES

way across it without dropping, and the children spend hours on it, especially on bad days.

My mother would be horrified to know I also let the children jump on the beds, especially in cold and wet weather. We just never have bought mattresses of such quality that it bothered me for the kids to jump on them. From the reaction of children who visit us, I must be the only mother around who allows this. At first I was afraid someone would get hurt, but we have never had a serious accident even after hours of play.

Hanging from our hayloft is a rope ladder that Shirley made. It is long enough that Booth can climb on the bottom rung and swing. The older children scurry up to the loft and drag the ladder up behind them to guard their clubhouse. Shirley insists you can tell the quality of a school by the way they use the space outside. Whenever we see a really neat play area, we stop the car and use it. Most people who are together enough to have an adventure playground are happy for others to use it if their kids are somewhere else.

I didn't get to the top of the monkey bars until I was twenty-seven, but most of my children made it by the age of two. Shirley gets the credit for this because I would not have had the courage to allow it without her. When a child begins to climb, she stands nearby so she can move to catch them in a second. They almost always get afraid coming down, but if she sees they can make it she encourages them by reminding them they went up. Sometimes she shows them where to place their feet, and every now and then she rescues them, but not often.

Music

It is difficult to tell whether we do music for me or the children. I'm one of those people who hum a tune all the time and break into song with the slightest provocation. I even hear songs when I'm using a push-button phone. If you call the farm from the apartment you get the first two bars of "It's A Small World After All."

All of this is to say that music is an important part of sharing with the kids. When they were infants, I used to cradle them in my arms and dance with them. Now we put on a fast record and dance in a pile. Hal likes "I Believe in Music," I like "I'm In Love With A Big Blue Frog," Julie likes "Free To Be You and Me," and Kelly loves "Frosty the Snowman." Booth's all-time favorite is "Jingle Bells." There are some records by Hap Palmer which are written just for young children. They are fast-paced movement songs that are fun to act out, such as "This Is the Way We Get Up in the Morning." We all enjoy his records and I really get into acting them out.

Several years ago I began a collection of instruments. We have tambourines, sand blocks, cymbals, bongo drums, bells, a recorder, an accordian, and a pump organ. We also have a mouth bow which no one can play and a dulcimer kit I can't assemble. The other night as the sun set and a full moon rose, Linda took her guitar outside and began to play praise music. I grabbed a tambourine and joined her, and before long each child had asked for an instrument. They would play awhile, then swap and play some more. We sang and marched and danced for about an hour. Booth hung in the whole time.

MUSIC

We expose the children to a variety of music and musical experiences. George likes country-western, Shirley prefers rock, and I enjoy folk, jazz and rock-and-roll. Unfortunately no one attends the symphony, but this year I plan to buy two tickets and try. We have taken the children to live performances of Handel's *Messiah* and *The Nutcracker Suite* when they were as young as three. I buy cheap seats because they are up high. The kids can see better and can get out in the aisle if they need to stretch.

Last year we took them to a ballet where Dame Margot Fonteyn was dancing excerpts from *Swan Lake,* and Hal and Kelly sat motionless. We also have seen the Osmonds, John Denver, and Larry Gatlin with the whole family. Denver is one of my favorites, and I play his records often so the children recognize and enjoy the songs. Even if they didn't, I believe that being included in group outings as a full-fledged family member would be a valuable experience. The many trips we take provide a good opportunity to sing together. I can't handle instruments in the car, but we sing *a capella* or with the radio.

The parks department in Nashville sponsors a movement and music class for four- and five-year-olds that is really good. Each class has a dance instructor and someone skilled with instruments. I have to drive fifteen miles to a park in a black housing project, and my blond girls are the only white children in class, but they truly love it, and it's worth it.

Last weekend the parks department put on a dance program at the Children's Theater. The music was written by and performed by the parks staff. Karen made a special trip to the farm to pick up the children so they could go. It was a really memorable experience for them to see their teachers dancing to music John and Tom had written.

Rainy-Day Excursions

It has rained a cold rain all day today. That reminded me of what a drag it can be to be in an apartment with four children on a bad day. There are, however, many things you can do to provide children a way to release energy. Shirley and I have a mental list of rainy-day excursions for city dwellers.

In Nashville there is a full-size replica of the original Parthenon in Athens. It is a beautiful building with a covered porch on four sides and an art gallery in the basement. On bad days we like to go there. The children run laps around the building and love it. Then they are usually ready to go inside and explore. Sometimes, we have a picnic in the car afterwards.

Another favorite place to go on rainy days is the Children's Museum. It has just moved into a new building, and it is chock-full of goodies for children. There is a two-story colonial dollhouse authentically furnished. There are areas set up where you can feel rocks and pelts. There is an animal show every hour, and they bring out a wild animal and tell you about its eating habits and the way it cares for its young. Also, there is a planetarium with a show for elementary-aged children. This place has free admission some days and is inexpensive the rest of the time.

One of our regular diversions for the winter months is to take the children to an indoor shopping mall. Many times there is some kind of exhibit or demonstration going on inside. Even if there isn't, it is

RAINY-DAY EXCURSIONS

warm and dry. We like to go window shopping and stop for a snack. It is easy to spend a couple hours in there at little or no cost.

One day this summer we were at the apartment; Craig was also there. It had been raining all day, even though the sun kept peeking through. I told the kids to go out and play, and they made a mass exit.

Thirty seconds later they reappeared and said, "It's still raining!"

I said, "I know; go play outside anyway."

For a minute they thought about feeling persecuted. Then they began to kick at the puddles. Next, they noticed the sailboat was full of water and began splashing each other. Soon the rain stopped and they asked for a bucket of water so they could continue their games.

Nearly all towns have a pet store. This is a fun place to visit on a bad day. Business is usually slow and the owner will probably spend some time letting you pet the animals. The airport is another public place with extra space and no noise rules. I love planes myself, and it gives me a lift to watch them take off. It seems to do the same for the kids.

Bad weather is not limited to cities. We have had some real adventures at the farm because of inclement weather. One morning I awoke there to find the earth shrouded with ice. The electricity was still on, and the phone still worked, but I was certain they would go out momentarily. The men were in town at work, and Shirley, Earline, the children, and I were stranded.

I called George to describe our predicament, and to find out how bad the storm was in Nashville. There was no storm in Nashville—only a light drizzle. I could tell he thought I was loony. Nevertheless I explained there was no way any of us could get out, and even if we could, the livestock would starve to death if we left them.

Next, I drove the four-wheel-drive vehicle a mile to Stayton and bought a gallon of kerosene for the lamps. Before we finished breakfast, the lights went off and an icy silence fell on the farm. Our water is pumped into the house from a spring, and with the electricity off, we were also without water.

We spent the next few days hauling hay, water, and feed to the cattle. On our first trip we discovered a newborn calf—dead—frozen to the ground. The ponds were frozen and every few hours we drew gallons of water from the spring and hauled them to the animals.

(This was a very good large-muscle activity!) We prepared our own meals in the fireplace and bundled up in two rooms to sleep.

George came bursting into the house around midnight of the first night. He had seen pictures of the storm on television and they had made a believer out of him. He had become frightened about our safety and had come to check on us. The closer he came to the farm, the more trees, lines, and stranded vehicles he encountered across the road. After numerous detours he finally got in. He agreed, once he was assured we were well, that we could not leave the animals, so after a warming cup of chocolate he went back to town.

On another occasion Shirley, Hal, Julie, Kelly, and Booth were at the farm when a heavy rain set in. As Craig and I drove out from town I felt some anxiety because I knew it had rained all night. I did not have the full grasp of what that meant until later that day. Craig and I observed that all the rivers and creeks had risen, and as we approached the farm we saw some out of their banks.

I felt some apprehension as I turned down the gravel road that leads to the farm. The puddles seemed to be deeper and there was a steady flow of water crossing the road in several places. I decided to approach the bridge slowly; if the water was over it I would turn back.

I eased my Volkswagen bus through a puddle and suddenly water gushed in through the clutch plate. The engine died and I could not restart it. In five minutes, a foot of water was standing in the bus. At first I was startled, because I knew the road wasn't that low here. I found out later that the road bed had washed out.

We decided to get out and see if there was anyplace to cross the creek. We stepped out of the bus in water up to my waist. Fortunately, I was holding the door handle because we found we were in the main current. We hauled our wet bodies back into the bus and began honking the horn, feeling very frustrated because we could see the barns and house, and yet were totally isolated.

Hal finally spied us and ran for Shirley. She came to the pasture across from us and told me to get out of the bus. She said the water had not yet crested. I chose not to believe her, and told her we would wait in the bus until we could cross over. Craig and I climbed to the far back of the bus, over the engine. He carried his guitar and I

RAINY-DAY EXCURSIONS

took my Bible. We were doing a fair job of cheering one another up until we realized the water was up to the rear window.

We waded back to the front of the bus and I opened the door on the driver's side. The current had become a torrent and almost pulled the door off. I held the top of the bus, stood on the armrest, and jumped onto a fence. I instructed Craig to do the same thing, and he jumped to me.

We had left our boots in the bus and the cold water numbed our feet. We pulled ourselves along the fence until we were out of the current. Then, holding hands, we began pushing through water almost up to our shoulders. (This was another excellent muscle builder.)

At one point Craig said, "I can't make it."

"You don't have any choice," I said. "WALK!"

Forty-five minutes later we stood exhausted on the front porch of the nearest farmhouse. The old people who lived there took us in, let us warm by their stove, fed us peanut butter and jelly sandwiches, and when the flood subsided, five hours later, drove us to a phone.

George made the trip from Nashville to the farm in record time. After he arranged for a wrecker to tow the bus out, we walked three miles across the back of the farm and brought Shirley and the children out.

I suppose the children could have been frantic, but they weren't. Shirley had moved them through their daily routine as if nothing unusual was happening. This was a feat in itself because the phone was dead, the electricity was off, and the wood was wet. She had broken up a chair to make kindling for the fireplace.

Shirley admitted to the children that we were in a predicament, but she was sure God would take care of us. She had come alone to the bank across from where we were stranded, and watched until she was sure we were out of the water. That evening when George, Craig, and I went in to get them, she had some warm soup ready for us. Each child had packed a small bundle and was patiently waiting to be rescued.

We have also spent some ordinary bad days at the farm. On rainy days we make extensive use of the barn. The kids go on picnics to the hayloft; they build houses of hay bales; they turn stalls into clubhouses. We also enjoy going to sales at the stock barn on inclement days. Once, I bought three sixty-pound pigs and loaded them right into the car with us.

Even if we don't go to buy, we all like to see the different sizes and kinds of animals. Booth loves baby pigs. Hal enjoys watching the buyers bid during the auction. Julie likes the Coke machine. There's something for almost everyone.

Small-Muscle Activities

A child's play is his work. He is a tireless worker. My responsibility as his parent is to offer a selection of activities which help him develop all the skills and concepts necessary to function as a whole person. Through play with puzzles, blocks, beads, sewing, and games, children deal with physical skills such as eye-hand coordination and visual discrimination; mental concepts such as size, shape, and sequence; and social skills such as sharing and being responsible for materials.

Nearly all toy manufacturers offer activities that teach colors, sorting, or sequence. When Hal was two, we bought a sorting box that looked like a poker-chip container. There were spaces for triangles, squares, circles, and hexagons, and each shape had a certain color. That toy lasted through three toddlers, trips, rain, pets, and several moves.

The children have all had stacking toys. Some of the earliest were the rings of different sizes and colors which fit on the cone, and wooden blocks which range from large to small and nest inside each other.

Our children are enchanted with blocks. We have alphabet blocks, colored blocks, design blocks, and cardboard and wooden building blocks. When Hal was two, he got a set of alphabet blocks in a small wagon which was the toy he played with most of that year. Booth has just come through a stage of intense block play. Whenever she got to select a toy she would ask for blocks. When we were at the Kendalls' she would head for Craig's closet and pull out the basket of unit blocks there. She even used the cuisinaire rods for blocks and could stack them to an unbelievable height before they would topple over.

One Christmas we found a set of plastic cubes which had a design on each side. The set had six different pictures of automobiles which could be put together with these cubes. They were neatly packaged in a small box, and Hal liked them well enough to haul the box back and forth between the farm and the apartment.

Each child has shown an interest in puzzles around the age of two. We buy only wooden or rubber puzzles for pre-schoolers. At first we find simple pictures with four or five pieces. When we can get them we select puzzles with a small knob on each piece, for this develops the muscles the child will use in holding a pencil.

The children are really neat with each other when they have a new puzzle. Whoever gets it first works it two or three times to make sure he can do it. Then when another child gets a turn he stands by to help. He doesn't try to take it away, but rather assumes the role of teacher.

Shirley and I keep most of the puzzles in the storage closet. Periodically we change the toys and give each child a couple of different puzzles. This keeps the children from getting tired of all of them at once.

We buy most of our toys at the local school-supply store. They usually have a wide selection of sturdily built playthings at competitive prices. We bought a set of beads there which have five shapes and a set of pattern cards to suggest ways to string them. The two- and three-year-olds are content to just get the bead on the string. The older children first identify the shapes, sort them into piles, and then follow the pattern cards.

Sewing is also a good activity for building eye-hand coordination. Even two- and three-year-olds can sew with the right materials. Shirley used to buy gutter wire, a pliable aluminum wire with quarter-inch holes, cut it into squares about twelve inches by twelve inches, and fold masking tape over the cut edges so the kids wouldn't get scratched. Each piece of prepared wire looked like a large pot holder with binding around it. She then wrapped a piece of masking tape around the end of brightly colored pieces of yarn, cut in one-foot lengths, to make stiff threads. The toddlers then wove the yarn throughout the webbing.

SMALL-MUSCLE ACTIVITIES

When they are around the age of four, we let the children sew pieces of loosely woven cloth such as burlap. We give them a large needle with embroidery thread in it, and usually define an area for sewing such as the table, so if the needle is lost we don't have to fear sitting on it. We also have some cardboard sewing cards with simple pictures on them. The threads are colored shoestrings with a good stiff point, and they can be unstrung and reused.

Last year, right before Christmas, Earline had her electric sewing machine set up in the trailer where she was doing the family mending. Hal and Craig began to pester her to let them sew saddlebags. She accommodated them with some scraps of material and careful instructions on how to sew a seam without including your finger. They spent an entire afternoon at the machine and grabbed everyone who came through to show them the finished product.

Our pre-schoolers started out with the *Hi-Ho Cherry* and *Sorry* games and have now moved into checkers, chess, and some rather hard card games. The other night they asked me to show them how to play *Parchesi*, and I was impressed that they allowed Booth to play with them. That meant every time it was her turn one of them had to show her which man it was to her advantage to move, and sometimes help her count it. As far as I could tell, they always gave her the best advice they could. She got tired of it before the game was finished and wandered off, but when she came back they let her take up where she had left off.

Although we de-emphasize competition around our house, we do realize that's how it is out in the real world. Along with teaching colors, counting, and other pre-reading skills, games offer children a chance to learn to play fair.

I somehow feel if you learn to play fairly with your brothers and sisters, you are likely to develop justice in your dealings with other people.

On the other hand, if you are allowed to reshuffle the cards, stop the game because you see you aren't going to win, move too many spaces, or take extra turns, you will find there is a way to get ahead even though you mess over others to get there.

Any time one of our kids attempts to play unfairly, he is simply excluded from the game. That's real life, too.

Sunny-Day Excursions

On pretty days we spend a lot of time outdoors. The first semi-warm day this spring, we made lunch and headed for the woods. We went up behind the spring and spread the meal on a pile of moss-covered rocks. After lunch we took pictures and collected wild flowers.

In warm weather we go swimming nearly every day. All the children are puddle ducks; so are the adults. There is a pool at the apartment and a lake nearby. At the farm we have a creek and several ponds. When we have been places where we didn't have access to any of these, we have used a small plastic pool or even a washtub.

Anything we have ever done inside with the children could have been done outside. We either take a child-sized table out or spread newspapers or a quilt in order to define a work area.

My children like to settle down under a tree and play a quiet game after lunch. All of us like to paint in the fresh air. Sometimes we tape paper to a fence or lay it on the ground and paint a mural. At other times we finger-paint or splatter-paint. Out of doors is also my choice for the woodworking area, especially if there is much hammering.

Sunshine makes Shirley a little crazy, and she usually comes up with some original ideas for play. One day she piled her VW bus full of milk crates and took some of the children from the Center to a large grassy area. When she got there, she threw the crates out on the grass and without a word, walked off a few yards and lay down. Soon the children were building houses, forts, and trains. They played this way most of the morning.

Sometimes we tape paper to a fence or lay it on the ground and paint a mural.

Karen used to take a load of toddlers from the Center to the car wash on pretty Fridays. They went to the kind where you ride through in your car. As the water, brushes, and burst of air engulfed them, the children would at first get wide-eyed and then break out in giggles.

Several times a year we take all-day excursions with the children. Sometimes we go to places close by such as Opryland. At other times we drive to the Memphis zoo, or the Space Center in Huntsville, or to Gatlinburg.

We went to Opryland the Friday before school started. Shirley and I had the children at the gate when it opened. I explained that each child should select one thing he really wanted to do, and I was going to select some shows for us to see. On the way into the park, I gave each child a dollar to spend on whatever snacks he wanted. It was a very special day. We alternated riding and going to shows. Shirley didn't have a certain ride or show picked out, so we ate Mexican food because that is what she wanted. We came home about four that afternoon and everyone scattered happily for quiet time.

We've gone to the Space Center the last two years. On the first trip I took Hal, Craig, and two other boys. We caught the Amtrak train in Nashville and rode to Decatur. There we rented a car and drove the twenty miles to Huntsville.

The exhibits at the center are designed to be superior learning experiences. There are about twenty different areas which focus on various parts of the space program. My favorite was the mock-up of the space lab. I could stand in there and get some idea of what it must be like actually to dwell in space.

Every thirty minutes they had a demonstration in a different area. We saw one on the difficulties of working in a state of weightlessness. Nose cones and space vehicles were hanging from the ceiling. There were games you could play with buttons and switches, and outside was a museum of many rockets including the Saturn V.

We caught the train home about four. The ride was as important to the boys as the Space Center. We had a snack in the dining car, then found some empty seats in the dome car and rode up there for a while. I hailed the conductor and told him it was the boys' first train ride, so he took them back to see his office.

As the children get older, the adults in our family seek them out with greater frequency for traveling companions. The child who gets to take a trip away from the other children has the benefit of lots of special attention. The adult who takes him is blessed by being able to experience events through the fresh eyes of a child.

At our place, planting a garden is an adventure. One planting day last spring about ten young adults showed up who had never been in a garden. Both they and the children learned many new skills that day. Hal and Julie were big enough to do some hoeing. Kelly found she liked to stick potatoes in the ground using a trowel. We gave each of them a stick the length of the desired space between each seed and everyone planted. Booth was still two years old then, but she followed the directions for planting very well.

Hal, Craig, and Julie kept the strawberry and asparagus beds weeded all summer. Sometimes they hoed and other times they pulled the weeds by hand. One of us always checked after they completed the task to see how they had done. Checking is important because it is positive reinforcement if they have done well and gives you a chance to correct any errors immediately if the task has not been satisfactorily performed.

One day, when the green peas came in, I headed to the garden with a basket on my arm. Booth wanted to go so I took her hand and we started down the road. I noticed she was carrying the baby Jesus from our nativity scene in her hand. As I began to pick she wanted to help, so I gave her handfuls of peas to carry to the basket.

She kept mumbling something about Baby Jesus and I noticed she had laid him in the basket so I said, "Is Baby Jesus taking a nap?"

She said, "No! Baby Jesus loves peas."

The children weeded all summer. I was concerned that we were drinking too many Cokes, so Shirley made a rule that the only way you could have a Coke was to work in the garden. It worked great. We usually assigned each child a row. Booth could tell a cantaloupe vine from a hogweed as easily as Craig. No one stayed with them but we did check on them. The only pressure was if they didn't finish, they didn't get a Coke.

Once this summer, we went to a farmers' market and sold vegetables and blackberries. For a couple of days before the sale, everyone picked and watched the pile grow. Shirley, Karen, and I took all four children and pulled our truck in right beside the other farmers'.

Suburban housewives descended on us. Hal helped make change while Julie and Kelly helped refill the berry baskets. Booth stood there and looked cute and drew a crowd. In forty-five minutes, we had sold out. I gave each child part of the money. Those who had picked berries got more than the others. We then went to a bookstore and spent every penny we had earned.

Traveling

Since the farm is fifty miles from the apartment, we have lots of experience on the road. We also usually take a thousand-mile trip to the beach twice a year. We try to remember on these trips that children are real people with real frustrations and a tremendous amount of energy. At every opportunity we take a romp. Sometimes we run three laps around McDonald's, or we'll race up a hill beside a service station, or pull over at a roadside park and play ball for a few minutes.

We spend more time preparing for long trips than we do taking them. We take many books on trips. Earline goes to the library before each trip and looks for subjects that relate to what we'll be doing. We hide part of the books, then swap them about halfway through the trip. It doesn't make me sick to read while riding so sometimes I read aloud to the children. We have read for over a hundred miles with each child picking a favorite book. Several weeks before a long trip we also begin to hide favorite puzzles, games, coloring books, and crayons. Just before we leave we get four small cardboard boxes and fill them with favorite activities for each child. Then as the children become restless, we pull out the boxes and let them explore.

Usually as vacation time draws close, I put the entire family (including Booth) on a diet. A diet means no soft drinks, potato chips, cookies, candy, chocolate milk, snack crackers, or other high-sugar or starch foods. The ban on junk usually lasts for two or three weeks and always ends as we leave for the trip.

The last time I did this, Shirley packed an empty lunchbox for each child. On the way out of town we stopped at a drive-in market and each one filled his lunchbox with snacks. Booth alone selected M & M's, peanut butter crackers, Certs, and something to drink. The other children also stuffed their boxes. They ate for the first hour we were on the road.

We also lift our ban on vending machines on trips, and I keep some change. At each stop the children pile out of the car to make a selection. After the initial shock, they don't even buy excessively.

We usually carry a cassette recorder in the car and pack the *Storyteller* tapes for the children. They rode the last hundred miles of a recent long trip listening to the tapes and looking at the books that go with them. We also take earphones so one child can listen if he wants to without disturbing the others. The children enjoy making original tapes and this is an excellent language development experience. A trip is a good time to let them do this because the finished tape can be kept as a souvenir of the family's time together.

We pack plastic cups, paper towels, and Wet Wipes on these jaunts. We also work out sleeping space for each child. A beanbag chair stuck in between the front and back seats of a car adds sleeping space. We put favorite pillows, blankets, and sleeping toys under the seat and distribute them at bedtime. When we pull them out, the children aren't tired of them and they recognize this signals a rest period.

If we want to go to a nice restaurant on a trip, we clean the kids up and go. On the way, I mention that it is time to find their restaurant voices. I carefully explain the use of napkin, utensils, and glasses. This is a great way to introduce new foods; we don't hesitate to share an unusual dish among the family.

We never tolerate bad behavior in any public place such as a restaurant, grocery, or shopping center. We will snatch up an ill-behaved child in a second and take him to the car. After we have explained why he was removed, we don't repent and take him back in to finish dinner. This is temporarily inconvenient because it means one adult has to be there, but it has a definite positive effect on both that child and the other children.

TRAVELING

Neither do we require the children to sit still very long after they finish a meal. The adult who finishes first takes them outside and lets them roam. Even I get a nervous twitch if I have to sit while everyone has dessert and coffee.

I confess that when I first began to have children I was not a very good traveling companion. My entire focus was on where we were going. I jumped in the car, demanded unreasonable calmness from children starched up to their necks, then expected everyone to have a good time when we got there. It took me a long time to realize that the value of a trip was not in just what we did at our destination, but also the kinds of experiences we shared along the way.

Waterplay

Waterplay can happen anytime and anywhere. Water can be poured, measured, weighed, colored, and splashed. It is always an excellent medium to use whenever the subject is cleaning. Babies begin waterplay with baths, and I've never met anyone too old to enjoy it. The one thing you can always count on is that people who play with water get wet. How wet usually depends on how much water. I plan ahead with a change of clothes and shoes, or take them off before play begins.

Shirley really likes to wash the truck. She changes shoes, gets a bucket of soapy water and a couple of rags, and goes to work. She always acts like she intends to wash the whole thing by herself. The first kid that comes along wants a rag, as does the next one and the next one. Before long there are kids swarming all over the truck. They don't horse around because they know she'll send them away if they do. They even clean the crumpled McDonald's bags out of the inside.

Booth was no more than eighteen months old when she began to wash dishes at the farm. She climbed on a milk crate beside me and quickly figured out it was okay to throw in the Melmac, but it was not acceptable to throw in the glass. Being able to make this kind of distinction is called sorting. I bought a sorting toy for seven dollars for the first three children. Booth practiced with dishes.

Next she got interested in pouring water from a cup to a bowl and back. She did this over and over—sometimes for an hour at a time—and always fussed when I finally rinsed what she was playing with. This pouring task is called measuring; the Montessori schools in our area which teach how to pour are very expensive, so Booth learned at the kitchen sink.

We have a creek which flows around the farm where we spend some time almost every day in the summer. Earline, Marilyn, Susan, and Karen are water-safety instructors, and all the children have learned to swim except Booth.

When Booth could just barely sit by herself she would sit in the creek and play with rocks. She regularly fell over, and she drank a lot of the creek that year, but there was always an adult nearby to right her and offer to move her from the water if she wanted out. She never did.

Craig has a two-man rubber raft and the kids and adults take turns pulling each other upstream and floating or paddling down. Sometimes they put it in the pond and paddle around watching the fish and turtles.

We take trash bags to the swimming hole to pick up beer cans the locals leave. The children usually play in the water with whatever container they find. When it's time to go home we fill the bags and throw them in the truck. Hal and Craig go through the trash when we get home and pick out the aluminum cans for recycling. We take the rest to the dump.

This summer, Shirley dragged a horse trough we weren't using behind the house so we could see it from the kitchen window. The kids put on their bathing suits and began filling it with water. They climbed in and out, splashed, jumped in, floated boats, and washed dolls.

Soon Shirley appeared with tempera mixed in liquid soap and some large paint brushes. First they painted themselves. Then they painted each other. My friend Liz who was visiting from Virginia with her two little boys seriously considered joining them. When they grew tired of the paint they just hosed each other down.

One of the favorite water games at the apartment is washing mirrors and windows. I guess all kids love those squeeze bottles—my kids will wash every glass thing in the house just to hold the bottle. It is important never to follow a child and redo what he has just done. Most kids are dead serious about the work they do, and it really puts them down to clean up behind them. Anytime the job needs to be done to meet my standard of perfection, I do it myself.

Little children always like to play in water. When Booth was about eighteen months old we would seat her at a table and put a large cake pan filled with water down on some newspaper in front of her. Then we would give her a box of water toys such as a medicine dropper, a syringe without a needle, small plastic bottles, and things that float such as boats, pieces of styrofoam, and little wooden people.

As long as I was working somewhere nearby or there were other children playing close to her, she would play all morning. If she got tired of the toys she had, I might give her a small doll with hair and a bar of soap and she again became absorbed in her work.

Of course, bath time is often waterplay time. The only place in the house I'll let the kids blow bubbles is in the tub. We have several boxes of waterplay toys which we rotate from time to time for use in the bathtub. The other night Booth asked to say the prayer at supper and one of the things she thanked God for was her water toys.

A waterplay task the staff often set up at the Center which was an excellent small-muscle activity used small clear plastic medicine bottles, two eye droppers, food coloring, and a small pitcher of water. They filled six of the bottles with colored water and put clear water in another bottle. With the droppers, the kids would then add two colors at a time to the bottle of clear water, and watch them blend into a third color. They then might add two more colors or pour that color out, add new clear water from the pitcher and try a new combination.

Also at the Center, Shirley would fill an eight-ounce plastic measuring cup with water and add a little food color. Then she put the cup, a funnel, and a small soft drink bottle on a tray and put it out where kids could get to it. I was amazed that some child was always involved in that activity. They would stand there and put the funnel in the bottle, pour the water in from the cup, pour it from the bottle back to the cup, and start over. They were learning visual discrimination and something about measuring, and they really were intrigued with it.

Woodworking

Woodworking is excellent for developing responsibility and safety-consciousness in children. Very young children can learn to properly use and care for tools if they are well supervised.

At the Center there was a woodworking area with a small table built from scrap lumber. It was very sturdy and the proper height for children. Hammers, nails, saws, screwdrivers, vices, and even electric drills were introduced to the children one at a time. The children were shown how to use them and where to place them when they weren't in use. Over the table was a sheet of pegboard with an outline drawn where each tool should hang.

Children who were usually disruptive and careless became responsible citizens in that area. They knew any deliberate infraction of the safety rules or misuse of the tools would mean they were banned from the table at least for that day and maybe longer.

We found a cabinet shop which would give away scraps of lumber. They supplied us with many interesting shapes and sizes, and much of it was soft wood. When Hal was six he built a small bench without any assistance. It didn't have perfect design, but he even braced it and is still using it in his room.

Even children as young as two can hammer nails. A small hammer, a pile of nails with large heads, and a piece of soft wood or fiberboard will entertain them for quite a while. This activity can be drawn out even longer if the toddlers are given something to nail to the board. Once, Shirley found some styrofoam disks about the size of a quarter which she let the toddlers nail to the wood.

As the children get older, they can apply bottle tops, ring washers, or other bits of wood. In addition to encouraging the proper use of tools, woodworking is an excellent activity for exercising the large and small muscles. It is equivalent to a jar of red paint in encouraging the child's creative expression.

Our children like to be creative with wood. They begin with a piece of wood approximately a foot square, or sometimes use an end from a two-by-four, and alternately apply glue and smaller pieces of wood. A box of assorted scraps and a large bottle of white glue will keep them occupied for a long time. They usually like to paint these creations with tempera. One of my favorite knickknacks is a small block of wood on which Kelly glued seashells.

In America, as technology has snowballed we have been presented with an increasing number of small appliances and other gadgets which are often discarded instead of repaired because we as consumers could not fix them ourselves. Many young adults are even ignorant of basic home repair skills. Introducing woodworking and the use of tools at an early age is one way to reverse that debilitating trend.

III

LEARNING ABOUT EMOTIONS

I first began to write this book as we sat around the table at the farm one night last fall. We had finished supper and the children had selected various tasks to work on as we sang. Because I was so full of joy, I began to write what was happening in order to release emotion. In the next three weeks, I basically completed the first two sections of this book.

Section three has taken six months to complete. In the introduction I stated that this part deals with areas of high emotional impact. That was an understatement. The treatment of each subject presented is not exhaustive; not all emotions a parent has to deal with are covered. For example, I never deal directly with children's fears.

However, the next few chapters have caused me to search the very depths of my soul. These are the emotions which have caused me problems. A series of before and after stories are presented; before Christ, and after Christ. My prayer is that not only will the examples throw light on problems, but that they will also offer troubled parents some alternative solutions.

Male and Female Created He Them

It seems a little strange to begin a chapter on the sex education of children in a Christian home by exploring the evolution of events which led to my own acceptance of my proper sex role. However, in this book it would be dishonest if I did not include such a discussion, because the search for my own identity has certainly affected the ways we have trained the children. This chapter will comment on the sexual preoccupation of our society and the way it affects our children. It will present a biased view of my perception of how most parents approach sex education in the home, and will then present the way we encourage healthy sexual development.

The decade of the seventies has been the era of the feminist movement. When the movement first began, any woman who aspired to a role which had formerly been dominated by males was immediately suspected of being sexually perverted or mentally unbalanced. It became clear during that period that many people identified which sex they were by what job they held. If a person of the opposite sex applied for the same job, their entire sexual identity was threatened.

I clearly identified and sympathized with many of the aggressive moves my female compatriots made. When I was twelve, my boyfriend showed me how to overhaul our lawnmower engine. From that day on I was the chief mechanic at our house. Even now my father probably doesn't know the difference between a chuck key and a socket wrench. From the time George and I married, I was the car mechanic, the plumber, and the handyman around the house.

I worked at many jobs in order to help pay for my education, and it's possible to list on one hand the men I respected because they were smarter than I. George was one of them.

It also seemed to me that girls were frequently better students than boys were, and that female professors were usually more interested in my development as a whole person than were the men. George's medical studies had revealed that girl babies survived better than boy babies, and that women could stand at least as much emotional stress as men could. The conclusion I drew from those facts was that women should receive equal wages and be given opportunities for equal jobs with men.

Interestingly enough, George agreed with me. He gave me his full support to tackle any job that appealed to me. As a result I taught school, worked as an assistant dietician in a hospital, taught an encounter group, ran a part-time nursery school, formed a corporation to bring tour groups into Nashville to see the Grand Ole Opry, worked in quality control for a construction company, went to an agricultural college to learn farm management, and applied to Vanderbilt's law school.

Shirley kept telling me I was missing it. She said the important things were going on at home with the children, while I was out flapping around. At the same time she was working on me, some of my Christian friends kept exposing me to the idea of being in submission to George.

As far as I could tell, neither George nor I felt like I was out of line. I kept looking at some of the men who got up to speak at church and was glad I didn't have to submit to them. George generally encouraged my aggressiveness, and I decided that unless I became convinced God said I was supposed to be in submission to some man, it wasn't anyone else's business.

Within a period of six weeks a series of events occurred which subdued me and caused me to realize God had said my place was to be one of submission.

First of all, George and I came to an impasse about educating Hal in a public school. I believed so thoroughly that we could give him a more challenging and wholesome education at home that I was willing to be stoned before I would give in about school.

George, on the other hand, was in the middle of a real financial mess which was causing him much mental anguish and a lot of hassle from official-type people. The possibility of one more problem with the system drove him up the wall. George stood his ground until he broke my will. I enrolled Hal in the second grade of the best school I could find, four weeks after the school year had begun.

Four weeks later, a doctor's wife from California came to our church fellowship and delivered a series of lessons on God's order for the family. I really liked the woman, but what she said gave me a headache. I took Earline to some of the lectures, and she got a headache, too.

When I finally accepted the role of helper and applied myself to that job full time, I really got blessed. First, I turned over all the household budgeting to George. I didn't like the tedium of paying bills, I had a tendency to overcheck, and it always made me nervous to know the money was low. I also discovered I was pretty tired of being equal, of being the person in charge, of answering irate phone calls, of always being behind, of having to look official all the time.

I found that if anyone wanted to yell at me I could refer them to George and he would shield me from the flack. I gave away my expensive, uncomfortable wardrobe and let George take me shopping for western clothes. I began to rock my children, and chase them through parks, and make cookies with them.

Two years ago I cringed at the thought of "just" being a wife and mother. I felt like I might smother if those were my only choices. Today, I am thriving in that role. I am now willing to cling to George and am proud to be one with him. Although it is still partly a mystery to me, I find that the more ways I can find to please him, the happier I am. I have learned to make eggs benedict from scratch because he likes it. I've taken to going to bed when he is tired just because he rests better if I'm there.

For George, the question of Hal's schooling was a legal matter. He did not demand that I become subservient to him. For me to give in on that point required a breaking of my will. The only philosophy I hold more important to me than how to rear my children is that a husband and wife are yoked forever. The only way I could have kept Hal out of school was to leave George, and I did seriously think about it. The day I decided to yield, I willed to serve him with as much love and consideration as I would give my dearest friend.

It is no mystery to me that he has become my dearest friend. It is a mystery only those who know God will understand, that George has grown from that day in humility, in wisdom, in gentleness, and in holiness.

I used to think giving up my rights as a woman would cause me to lose my individuality and self-respect. I loathe women who are mousey, and was afraid I would become like them. After committing myself to submitting all my decisions to George, there was no indication I would like the person I was to become. I acted on the faith that God is a loving Father and would respond to my obedience by giving me a bearable self-image.

I like the person I am becoming. For a while the growing gentleness of my spirit scared all of us. Shirley even took a couple of days off work to see if she could irritate me to the point of anger. I was so quiet she wasn't sure it was me. It has taken some time for everyone to learn I refer all points of conflict to George. I used to personally mediate all family problems, and tried to shield George from any crisis. Now I go straight to him. Just the knowledge that George is going to find out has cut out a lot of trash.

I do not accept the idea that the house is my only domain, and that I'm intruding every place else. The whole earth is my domain, and I probe and search it from every possible posture. I bore Julie by natural childbirth because I wanted to experience the total spectrum of the pain and pleasure of giving birth. This fall I tore down and rebuilt the chimney in my kitchen because it needed it, and because I had never done that before. Driving a tractor makes me feel powerful. Chopping wood for my stove gives me a feeling of kinship with all the pilgrim women who chopped wood to help keep their families alive.

God predestined George's role as head of the household at the moment of his conception. He predestined my role of submission at my conception. However, we both parent, we both string fences, and we both kneel to pray. We teach our children they have defined

MALE AND FEMALE CREATED HE THEM

manhood or womanhood by nature of their birth, but we place no limitations because of their sex on how they develop as individuals.

We have taught our children that the act of sex is holy, not dirty. In Gen. 1:28 the Creator God spoke His first words to the newly created man and woman. He said to them, "Be fruitful and multiply, and fill the earth. . . . " Many conclusions could be drawn from the fact that these were God's first recorded words to man. The point I would like to dwell on is that I don't think He spoke this command with a blush on His face and His hand over His mouth.

The proportions of distortion and perversion in which twentieth-century man has carried the simple act of mating are limited only by man's imagination. Advertising companies use sex to lure us to buy everything from toothpaste to automobiles.

Many parents deal with sex and all related topics with such secrecy that the most naive child is made curious. They dangle the subject like candy in front of their children's faces. They take great care to hide the *Playboy* in the closet. They shut doors or speak in whispers even when talking about a visit to the doctor. Then they dress in something slinky and ask the first adult who comes along if they look sexy.

Children are bombarded with mixed messages about sex. It is exciting, but it is dirty. Everyone seems to know about it, but no one will talk about it. Parents, peers, and the media send out messages about sexy cars, sexy music, and sexy aftershave. No wonder more and more young adults are gravitating toward bi-sexuality or unisex. They have picked up the message from their environment that everything important is tied to sex, but no one will define for them the difference between a man's role and a woman's role.

The illusions all suggest that being submerged in sexy things makes one happy. The current divorce rate, abortion rate, and suicide statistics indicate that young people have been deceived about sex. "What can sex do for you?" is a mystery that man created. God's plan is that each individual is born either male or female. The implication from the verse in Genesis is that this is to facilitate procreation. God also had the grace and forethought to throw in pleasure as a by-product of the mating process.

I personally believe every child has a natural, healthy curiosity about his own body and sexuality. He is interested in the likenesses and differences between his sex and the sex of his siblings and peers. A little boy notices and wants to talk about the differences in appearance of his body and the body of his father. When a toddler points and says, "What's that?" we give him the proper scientific name, such as vagina, penis, or breast. As children mature and ask more complicated questions about sex-related topics, we give them the most complete answer they are capable of understanding. We try not to burden them with information they don't ask for.

The fact that we have given each child a scientific vocabulary about his body almost got Hal kicked out of playschool when he was three. He was in a church-sponsored, half-day program, and some subject came up which involved the navel. Hal simply stated the correct word was umbilicus. The teacher said the word was navel and became very distraught when Hal wouldn't give in. I knew that very day we had better begin seeking educational alternatives for our children.

One thing all parents need to realize is that all children play doctor so they can take their clothes off and peer at each other. I suppose that since we are a medical family, our children play with a little more sophistication than others, but that is the only difference. I always keep my ears open to make sure the sex play doesn't get out of hand. Whenever a child indulges in sex play in public, I make the comment that the child's room is a more appropriate place if he feels like he needs to do that.

I don't believe this matter-of-fact approach encourages deviation. A four-year-old is going to be curious about his body whether I approve or not. If I tell him his curiosity is dirty, that does not kill his interest. It only encourages him to hide all further explorations from me, and lays a guilt trip on him. I much prefer to maintain the kind of communication with the child which lets me give approval for appropriate behavior.

When I was four, I played doctor with the little boy across the street on my neighbor's front porch. My mother discovered us and spanked me soundly. I still see him occasionally, and the first thought that crosses my mind is, "Does he remember us taking our clothes off?" If he does, he has always had the grace not to let me know. I really appreciate that because I feel guilty anyway. I imagine that had the incident gone unnoticed, I wouldn't even remember it. I never moralize with the children about sex play by using words such as *bad, ugly,* or *shameful.* I simply point out there are times and places when sex is appropriate and times and places when it is not.

Since we live on a farm with animals, the children understand that those who mate, procreate. They have made the jump that people who mate have babies. We have told them that it is God's plan that intercourse occur within the institution of marriage.

They also know that some people choose to disobey God's will in this. We had an unwed mother who lived with us before and after her baby was born. She had regular nightmares about giving the baby up for adoption. We kept a baby boy for a while whose single mother wanted to keep him, but she was so tied up in guilt and anxiety that she had trouble functioning as a mother. We offered emotional support and a safe place for the baby when she was about to lose it.

We have gotten up in the middle of the night for George to diagnose the acute pain in the pelvis of an eighteen-year-old drug addict as venereal disease. We have prayed for Daddy as he sat for three days beside the bed of a fifteen-year-old who gave birth to a child and then nearly bled to death from disseminated intravascular coagulation.

It isn't necessary for me to turn these events into horror stories to teach my children morals. They have been there as these things happened, and they know they hurt the people involved. My role has been primarily to soften the blow by assuring them that God can reconstruct any life given over to Him.

In addition to not teaching the children that sex is dirty, we have carefully avoided designating toys, clothes, emotions, or work tasks as girl things or boy things. All the children cook and sew; all of them cut wood and haul rocks; all of them get cuddled. Crying is not limited to the girls, and aggressiveness is not just something boys do. Hal asked for a Pooh bear for Christmas; Kelly wanted a motorcycle racetrack. They each received what they asked for.

I teach the children not only that is Daddy the boss, but also that my first concern and duty is to please him. The answer for why I do many things a certain way is because Daddy likes it that way. The children take turns sitting to his left at the supper table, and that child waits on him for that meal.

When George is gone, Hal often asks to sit in his chair and I let him. We don't wait on Hal, but he and the girls know he will be the God-appointed head of his own home some day. This simple form of role-playing encourages him to develop the virtues of gentleness, patience, and mercy which are a part of every true leader. We also use those times when he is playing daddy to teach him the difference between chauvinism and leadership.

In selecting and eliminating goals for themselves, children play many roles. They also work through fear and other conflicts during times of make-believe. Role playing may take many forms—puppets, doll play, acting out parts in costume. Toy dealers offer elaborate appliances, kits, and even pre-fab play houses because they know children enjoy this kind of play. The three recurring roles I keep hearing being acted out at our house are baby, doctor, and school.

The most interesting thing about the way they play is the role Booth takes. Since she was two, the children let her assume any role. If she wants to be mama, they will be the baby. Should she choose to be teacher, they will be students.

Recently, Booth and Kelly built a block house in the Kendall's living room and invited Earline to be the baby. She told them she was sorry, but she wouldn't fit in the house. They extended the blocks to the sofa and told her she could be the baby on the sofa.

When Hal and Craig are together, they drag out their tractors and play elaborate farming games. If the girls want to play, they get assigned to cultivate the beans in the north forty, or some similar tasks. Each child participates in each role, and I am fascinated that they let Booth have so much choice.

She and Hal play the melodrama where Booth is the landlord and Hal's rent is due. She says, "But, you have to pay the rent!"

He replies, "But I can't pay the rent!"

They say this four or five times, almost in a chant, and then she says, "Why can't you pay the rent?"

Hal offers, "Because I don't have any money!"

Then they both break up in peals of laughter.

Given total freedom of choice as to toys they play with, roles they assume, tasks they work at, clothes they wear, and emotions they display, our children have made some interesting decisions. Hal has become a football nut.

When you consider we have never encouraged competitive play or any kind of physical aggression, I think it is amazing that Hal has focused on football. Even before he started going to public school, he began pestering me to take him to a football game. I told him that when he could sit still for an entire game on television, we would buy him a ticket.

In an eighteen-month period he has become a walking statistics book on each player and every game played in the past ten years. He asked me yesterday if I knew that Fran Tarkenton had a little girl born in 1963. This school year he has checked out every book in the school library relating to football. He made elaborate arrangements with me during the season of Monday night football so he could watch the games and still get his rest time in.

Each child selected two toys for Christmas, and Hal chose Pooh and football gear. Although most of the adults in the family enjoy watching the games, none of us have encouraged Hal to actively participate. I did comment that if he is going to play I hope he will be a kicker so he won't get mauled, but his interest leans toward the positions of center or safety.

As far as I can tell, his friends at school aren't even much interested in the game. I hear him talking about them playing baseball, but football seems to be his own thing.

Julie has chosen to be a little lady. I am very comfortable in faded jeans, but I support Julie's right to focus on fashion. She wanted a Barbie Beauty Center for Christmas and we got her one. Although I gave up make-up the year after Julie was born, I carefully showed her how to apply false eyelashes, rouge, and lipstick to Barbie.

Julie's fascination with clothes, jewelry, and cosmetics makes me slightly uncomfortable, but I have allowed her to explore any facet of our made-up culture that she chooses. She has a full wardrobe of dainty, fashionable clothes she selected herself. She also has some really ragged-looking play clothes she sometimes wears to school. I make sure she knows how to care for her shoes and clothes, how to file her fingernails and apply polish, and which piece of jewelry looks best with the outfit. She checks with me to see if she looks all right, and I give my full approval when she does, and make suggestions when she doesn't.

I cannot imagine how she got so absorbed in fashion. The only model she has for this in the extended family is Earline, but while Earline has class, she doesn't dwell on fashion. My mother is the only adult who regularly encourages Julie in this direction. She doesn't see enough television to be influenced by it, and we don't subscribe to the newspaper or any magazines which carry fashion ads. I've noticed Julie's peers and classroom teachers all wear jeans or pantsuits, so she hasn't been influenced by them.

The conclusion I must draw from what I've seen in my children thus far is that if children are given free choices in the roles they will assume, their lives will unfold according to the designs God placed within them. That does not mean all little boys will grow up to be football players and all little girls will grow up to be Barbie dolls.

It does not even mean they will grow up to be mothers and fathers. The Bible clearly teaches in 1 Corinthians 7 that some men and women have a God-given gift of being single. Our family includes several single men and women who live lives full to overflowing. They regularly wash the adults and the children in their gift of love, and we fill their need to be part of a family.

I do believe man was created in the image of God. Not only within every man is there a yearning for God, but there is also a potential blueprint for growth according to God's plan. So much of what we have taught our children about sex and sex roles is cultural, not scriptural. The only way any child can grow into wholeness as an adult is through the power of the resurrected Christ. If we, as parents, can stay out of His way, He will be faithful to complete the work He has begun.

Blessed Are the Dead Who Die in the Lord

My grandmother, Mama Jaynes, died this past October.

She had never seen my children because she went blind when I was sixteen. She was a really special person who dealt with blindness more positively than anyone I have ever known.

All my memories of her are warm. I used to drop by for lunch and she would feed me a hamburger patty with mustard on top and cold green beans. She could play a harmonica like a professional and last year right before her ninety-sixth birthday she played "Listen to the Mockingbird" for the children. She was so alert that she knew about fifty phone numbers by memory and recognized the voices of most of her one hundred and fifty descendants. She used to ask me, "How's your kosporosticgaspurating?" or tease me in some other way.

From the time Hal was born I took my family to visit her. When they were tiny babies she would hold them and tell them she wished she could see them. When they got to be about two and a half, they would be afraid of her because she was bent over and wrinkled and talked a little loudly.

Gradually, each child discovered her charm and warmth for himself. Before she died, all of them but Booth would plop down beside her and lean across her lap. They would take her items they had made and tell her about them. She liked to feel their hair, and if they were wearing something special they would let her touch it. For the last two Christmases, Linda had taken her guitar and gone out to her house with us to sing carols. We would sing hymns and she would cry softly and clap her hands when we finished.

We were at the beach the week before she died. I dreamed she was dying, and we packed and came home expecting her to be gone. A week later she did die. She passed away quickly and I was thankful she did not have to suffer. The funeral was in Kentucky, and George and I let Hal and Julie go with us. I explained to both children how joyful I was she was with Jesus, that it must be really neat for her to see again. I told them part of the family would probably cry a lot because they would really miss her. We impressed upon both of them that to feel lonely because someone had died was a natural feeling, but that mostly we were going to celebrate her arrival in heaven.

The service was truly a witness of how Jesus Christ in the heart of this one little lady had touched so many lives. Several people spoke of how she had taken them in and been a mother to them when they really needed one. Hal and Julie were really moved and both of them cried briefly. I just wanted to break forth in praise to God for His care of her and his mercy in taking her so gently.

I suppose some people think I am irreverent about death. The truth is, if a Christian dies, I view death as a time of celebration. If the deceased was not a Christian, I see it as a time to minister to that family.

I *am* irreverent about funeral homes. I think most of them coerce families into spending money they usually don't have in order to buy a box which is supposed to be a witness of how much they loved the deceased. I think it is absurd that if one of our family died today we couldn't bury them under the big cedar tree at the farm because that is against the law.

George and I have written into our wills that at death we want all healthy organs made available for transplant, and what is left of the body sent to a medical school. My idea of an ideal funeral would be for all the people who loved me to gather in front of a warm fire, share cider and popcorn, and sing some of my favorite songs.

We have always dealt with the subject of death very matter-of-factly with the children. We chose to expose them to death and the rituals of death in our culture at an early age. To do this, we let them attend funerals of several older people they had visited occasionally, but were not emotionally involved with.

This past spring Earline's father died. The children had met him once or twice, and the night before he underwent surgery we took them by to see him. The two months following his surgery the family expected anytime to receive the news that he had died.

The night Hal's colt was born, Earline and Jay were called to town by the doctors. Still he lingered, to the point that he wanted to die. At first, the doctors had given the family hope he might recover, but now even they had given up hope that he would.

None of us were shocked when he passed away.

George took the day off to attend the funeral so the kids understood that for some reason we needed to be supportive. We gave the three older children the option to attend the funeral if they wanted to. Hal didn't want to dress up so he stayed home, but Kelly and Julie went.

As soon as we got to the chapel, Kelly sat down beside Earline and said, "Where's your daddy?"

Earline pointed to the casket and said, "His body is in that box."

Then Kelly wanted to know how they got him in there and if there was a pillow inside. Earline told her there was a pillow but he couldn't feel it because he was dead.

Julie wanted to know why they had those *weeds* on top of the casket. She was told that the leaves were called a pall and most caskets had some kind of pall on top.

By this experience, the children were allowed to view death as casual observers. They received information which answered some of their questions about death, without having to be emotionally involved.

Almost every child goes through the experience of having a pet that dies. To a small child, a beloved pet is just as much a part of his real world as are his parents. For that reason, it is important that the child receives accurate information as to how or why the animal died. If he is deceived at this point, he will discern that information is being withheld, and his anxieties about his parents or other important people leaving him are likely to increase.

It is also important for him to receive emotional support during the crisis. The child experiences the same kind of grief we adults would feel if our best friend died. It isn't necessary for the entire household to be disrupted by the death of a pet, but if the child wants to skip a couple of meals, his feelings should be considered.

On Hal's sixth birthday his puppy was run over. I had gone to gather party paraphernalia, and the children had gone on an outing with their grandparents. When I got home and learned his puppy was dead, I was stricken with grief.

As soon as he came in the door, I took him to my bedroom, held him in my arms, and told him about the accident. He burst into tears and I held him until he sobbed it out. He wanted to know what had happened and what we had done with the puppy. I explained he had slipped through the fence and wandered into the road. One of our teen-age foster sons had buried him in the back yard before I got home.

Although I was relieved the puppy was buried, had I been there when it happened I would have waited for Hal to come home and let him participate in burying the dog. George told him that he could have another puppy. Julie told him they could share her puppy, a sister to Hal's pup.

Because he was given the simple facts as soon as possible and then was allowed to fully vent his hurt with family support, I believe he pulled himself together much more quickly then he might have.

Some deaths, particularly the death of a child, are especially disturbing to children. The most traumatic death our children have experienced was the kidnaping and murder of a little girl in our town last spring. I suppose all the children in town were terrified—it was in the media for days. Although I answered all their questions as honestly as possible, it still took a long time for them to work out their fear. Julie wrote the parents a letter of consolation. Kelly named her doll after the little girl, and Hal had a nightmare that he was kidnaped.

Until the body was found, the parents stood in faith that she would return safely. When the bad news came, they confessed they did not understand it, but they believed God would use it to His glory.

The gossipmongers in this town went berserk. They could not bear such a witness of affirmation that God is in control. Upon those parents' heads, already bowed low with grief, were heaped condemnations and accusations that they were involved in the tragedy. I was appalled at the community response. For a couple of weeks I didn't take the kids to any public place except church and school. Even then I had to listen as they worked through tons of trash.

The truth is—yes—it could happen to them. The rest of the truth is that the adults in our family are very protective of the children. Unless the kids are in bed, they are almost never out of the watchful eyes of one of the adults. This is especially true if we are in town. We prayed with the children that God would surround them with an angel guard. We went over our rules for not going in other people's houses without first checking in at home, not stopping to talk with strangers in a car, and not telling a phone caller whether Dad is at home or not.

Gradually, the fear lifted. While it had been with us, I was careful not to *suppose* anything. I gave them all the information I had and we shuddered through it together.

I remember, as a child, whenever something morbid happened involving a child, the adults always protected me from the details of the incident. Before I was able to read, voices would drop to whispers when I entered a room. After I could read, there was much bustling around to hide papers or magazines which contained horror stories. All of the secrecy made me really afraid. I sensed something awful was going on and fantasized that whatever *it* was might get me next. I couldn't discuss my fears because I wasn't supposed to know anything was wrong.

I decided to give my children an alternative to that dilemma.

In June of this year a friend of ours who was living as a Christian minister in a New York ghetto was shot and killed. He was a brilliant young man and his enthusiasm for life attracted all who knew him. On the Wednesday night after he was killed, our church held a memorial service in his honor. Many of his friends shared ways he had influenced their lives. They talked of his devotion to the Lord and his compassion for the underdog. Someone asked that we sing "Tempted and Tried" because it was one of his favorite songs.

When our minister first called me to tell me of Phil's death he said, "Our brother Phil has already made it." The service at church clearly affirmed we believed Phil was with our Lord. The children asked me why God let someone who was just twenty-eight and trying to live for Him get killed. My reply was that the Bible clearly teaches that some who love the Lord will have to die for Him. Phil was one of the few of us who had the guts to do that.

Last week one of Phil's co-workers in the ghetto visited our congregation and shared how the people in that New York slum had begged them not to leave. He told how they had more support from the neighborhood and more interest in Jesus than they ever did before Phil was killed. When they passed the basket to collect money for the program, Hal put in his only dollar—his granddaddy had given it to him as a gift.

The children first had to deal with death as God's will for Phil. They now have begun to see it as a witness to all of the people whose lives he touched. Blessed are the dead who die in the Lord.

A Heritage of the Lord: Handle with Care

All parents, teachers, and other keepers of children are regularly called upon to administer first aid or to care for an ill child. The skills and information necessary to carry out this function with confidence are attainable for most people who want to learn them.

Although George is a doctor, he does not practice medicine on the children. Under pressure, he will look at a sore throat with a flashlight, but all other medical care of the children is left up to me. I have always been interested in first aid, and I once took a basketball-team-trainer course by mail, but the rest of my knowledge is the result of a mixture of curiosity and common sense.

This chapter is divided into two parts. First, there is a discussion of the care of major and minor injuries. The latter half of the chapter concerns the child who is ill.

Accidents can happen in any family. The preventive training we give our children includes many instructions about how to avoid accidents. We have always tried to lock up medicines, poisons, and dangerous tools. Some of our strictest discipline is centered on teaching the children to climb steps properly, to stay out of certain drawers, and to leave wall plugs alone. Still, we have had accidents which demanded immediate medical care.

When Kelly was two, she fell from the top of a stairwell, off the side, and received a severe blow to the mouth. George and I, and two other adults were in the house at the time. Kelly had been taught to climb the stairs on the side next to the wall, but in an attempt to go around Hal, she fell or was pushed off. (A year after the accident, Hal said she stepped on his puzzle and he pushed her. She maintained she just fell.)

Whatever happened, Kelly's mouth was a real mess. I immediately sent the other children to another part of the house so their reaction to her appearance would not frighten her. George got on the phone and made arrangements to meet an oral surgeon. We wrapped ice in a clean washrag, held it against her mouth to try to control the blood loss and swelling, and left to meet the doctor.

She lost two teeth, knocked two others loose, and bit a hole through her bottom lip. The dentist said there was nothing we could do except give her Tylenol for pain.

The next morning when we brought her to breakfast, her face looked terrible. We had discussed her injury with Hal and Julie, and asked them not to stare at her or ask her if she hurt. We offered her cooked cereal. She asked for bacon, and ate it. I couldn't believe a mouth like that could possibly chew bacon, but she never hesitated.

A good thing to remember whenever there is an accident is that kids are really tough.

Injuries that require a doctor's care don't happen very often. Since most of the mishaps we deal with are minor, we treat them casually. If a two-year-old falls down and skins his knee, we urge him to jump up. We seldom pick him up. Since we act like he ought to be okay, he usually is.

If the child begins to cry, we tell him that when he quits crying he can tell us where it hurts. If the child tries to say where it hurts through the tears, we declare we can't understand him because he is crying. When he manages to say clearly what happened and what hurts, we apply appropriate first aid and compassion.

We use large numbers of Band-Aids. They are a visible sign that we realize the child had some discomfort. We call the scabs that form later "God's Band-Aid," and the plastic Band-Aids stay on until God puts His on. After treating the wound, we usually hold the child for a minute, then offer him something to drink and send him on his way.

You are okay is an attitude a parent can transmit to the child. The child soon learns to judge for himself that he is okay. While he may report minor injuries in order to gain a moment of attention, he won't turn every scrape into an episode.

The attitudes and behaviors a child exhibits when he is sick or injured are learned directly from the adults who care for him. Anytime I see a child go into hysterics at the sight of blood, I'm eager to see what his parent is like. Fifty years ago, a child who was bleeding badly was in danger of dying. Today, it isn't likely a child will bleed to death.

Whether or not the child is afraid when he cuts himself depends on whether or not his parents have taught him to be afraid. The child needs all the support he can get from his parents because our society is enraptured with blood and gore.

Unthinking inquirers often transmit unnecessary fear or fascination with the injury. Booth has a black eye right now from running into an iron rail. It is amazing how total strangers react to injured children. They walk up to the child and say, "Oh honey, how did you hurt yourself?" That is supposed to be a cue for me to answer how she hurt herself. I usually don't play the game, but just stand there. If Booth knows she is hurt and wants to talk about it—fine. If she doesn't, we both stare blankly at the nosey person.

Not only do parents transmit their own fears about injuries and sickness to their children, but also they transfer a fear of the doctor. Anyone who observes the behavior of many children in the doctor's office knows this is true.

It is possible to prepare a child so he knows what to expect and how he is supposed to react, thereby lessening his trauma. Any time one of our children is ill, we discuss what the probable treatment will be before we get to the office. If it is likely the child will be given an injection, we tell him so. We discuss carefully any methods of diagnosis or treatment the doctor may use which will hurt. We clearly state that it will hurt, but that we expect the child to keep himself under control.

We don't promise ice cream or balloons for good behavior. A child who is frightened is not likely to be bought out by ice cream. We try to convey the message that what is going to take place is bearable and we know the child is mature enough to bear it.

One day after being thoroughly prepared in that manner, Julie started crying loudly when the doctor came into the room. Since she had never acted that way before, I assumed we were not dealing with fear, but rather the issue of whether she or I were in control. I told her I would come back into the room when she got herself calmed down, but would not stand there and watch her cry. I walked out of the room and shut the door, leaving her with the doctor and nurse. Two minutes later all crying had ceased, and I returned to the room and told her how much better it felt for her to be quiet.

A parent who lies to the child about what to expect and then tolerates an episode of bad behavior leaves the child in an emotional dilemma. He is afraid of something he can't define and his parent won't help him to gain control of the situation.

It is not that I'm unsympathetic with the child's pain; it is just that I know a cooperative child is much easier to treat than one who is screaming.

We have been blessed to have two good pediatricians. When each child was born, Dr. Wheeler came to the hospital and told me all about the condition of the baby. He encouraged me to ask questions and took time to write down the answer to every question. By the time Booth was born I knew more answers than questions!

When we moved one direction and Dr. Wheeler moved the opposite, we started going to Dr. Laird. He is a soft-spoken man with kangaroos appliquéd to his lab coat.

Both Dr. Wheeler and Dr. Laird seem to genuinely enjoy children. Each speaks to the children as little people instead of objects. I absolutely believe they are competent and I'm willing to follow their directions to the letter. If they were rude to the children, or if we didn't trust their medical judgment, we would choose someone else.

I'm appalled that some parents take their child to the doctor, pay for the office visit, pay for the medicine, and then don't follow the doctor's directions for treating the illness.

I've heard mothers say they couldn't get their child to take his medicine. Those parents obviously don't understand how important it is to give it like it's prescribed. Show me a child I can't give medicine to, and I'll show you the Jolly Green Giant.

On the radio the other day it was stated that one out of five deaths in the United States is from kidney disease. I'm guessing that at least half those deaths could be avoided if mothers followed doctors' orders.

An ill child will be taken to the doctor and the diagnosis will be a

A HERITAGE OF THE LORD

bladder infection. The doctor will write a prescription which clearly states it is to be taken *until it is gone*. He probably also tells the mother to bring the child back after he finishes the medicine so the urine can be checked to see if the infection has cleared.

Mama has the prescription filled and gives it diligently for two or three days. By then the child appears to be much better so she decides she won't give him any more of that high-powered medicine. Neither does she get around to taking him back to the doctor.

The child has been given the medicine just long enough to really irritate the disease bacteria. Although the symptoms may appear to be better, the infection is just beginning to fight. The next time the child becomes ill with similar symptoms, the infection has moved from the bladder to the kidneys. If Mama treats the illness this time as casually as she did before, she has usually passed a sentence of kidney disease on her child.

Although we treat illness with respect, we try to keep it in proper perspective. A child with an earache doesn't need to be in bed unless he wants to nap. A child with pneumonia doesn't need to be up except for brief quiet periods.

Just because someone is ill doesn't mean life has to stop for everyone else in the house. We allow the other children to pursue any plans they have already made. That constant activity helps the child who is ill to want to get well more quickly. We want them to feel it is more fun to be well than sick. Many children only get the attention they need when they are sick. Those children often grow up to be hypochondriacs.

This is not to imply we all go off and leave the sick child with a babysitter. Either George, Shirley, or I stay home with the patient. We are all sensitive to bedroom boredom and are willing to spend time reading or listening to music or watching television with the child. If the child is very ill, each of us is comfortable that we would recognize signs that he was getting worse and could decide what to do next.

The children all trust us and know we are capable of taking care of them. Since we deal with the children in a straightforward manner about pain, they also believe us when we tell them they will be well soon. Sick children sometimes need this word of comfort from an adult they trust.

Many adults live under a cloud of mental anguish because they don't believe they are really well. Although various doctors pronounce them in good health, they believe there is something seriously wrong with them that no one is telling them. These people are also hypochondriacs. If a loving parent had transmitted the attitude that "you are going to be well soon, and when you are we need to do thus and such" they would probably be much happier adults.

I suppose each of our children has faked an illness at one time or another. We have a special treatment for that disease at our house. We follow the same course of treatment we would use if he were sick, minus the medicine.

If he fakes stomach trouble we don't feed him for a day, and we usually take the other kids to buy ice cream. No amount of assurance from him that he is better will procure for him an ice cream cone. If he fakes a headache we suggest a nap and restricted activity. Should the symptom be an earache, he can't go swimming or get out in the wind to go somewhere.

The reason we have the nerve to do this is because we always take any suspicious illness to the doctor. We never ignore a fever, or complaints of a sore throat or earache. Once we know we've been tricked, we offer the healthy children so many good choices that the faker doesn't pull that trick again.

This brings me to "school phobia"—a topic I didn't intend to discuss. Just this week I read an article about how to treat school phobia. Yesterday, in Dr. Laird's office, I noticed he had printed instructions for how to deal with this *illness*.

Apparently it is on the increase. The cause is given as an unwillingness to leave home or mother. The symptoms run the gamut from headache and dizziness to nausea and vomiting. The patient is said to feel much better soon after the school bus passes his house.

The suggested treatment is basically to ignore the symptoms and force the child to go to school. The instructions also caution the parent against going to school in the middle of the day to bring home a child who is supposedly ill.

I'm sure there are times when the suggestions the doctors offered are the only way a family can deal with school phobia. This is especially true if both parents work or if it is a one-parent household. I do need to point out, however, that whenever a physically healthy child would rather be at home all day than with other children,

A HERITAGE OF THE LORD

something is very wrong. The child is indicating that something at school is causing him so much mental anguish he would rather hide than deal with it. Kids are tough. If they are so distressed that they can't cope with the problem themselves, then someone who loves them needs to lend support.

Bear Ye One Another's Burdens: Alternatives for Dealing with "School Phobia"

When Craig was in fourth grade he developed "school phobia." Earline was working every day, so most of the time staying home from school meant he would be alone. The symptoms were especially acute if anyone were going to be at home. This phobia continued into the fifth grade, and the language arts teacher insisted Earline have Craig tested. Even though he couldn't write a complete sentence, Earline was so wary of him being labeled that she refused to put him through a battery of tests.

By the time Craig finished fifth grade, Earline was directing the Children's Center. I was on the board of directors, all four of my children were enrolled there, and I spent most of my time at the Center. When the lawyer had written its charter, we had asked him to word it so the Center could eventually be an alternative elementary school. I had looked all over town for a public or private school that I felt represented my philosophy of education. There just wasn't any, so I had in mind "rolling my own."

During the summer I began to work with Craig and some of the other older children on an informal basis. When school opened that fall, the Kendalls held Craig out of sixth grade and we held Hal out of first.

Craig's first assignment was to watch "Electric Company" a

minimum of three times a week. Hopefully he could start learning to spell by doing this. Then he was told I would not accept any written communication from him until after Christmas. He could make notes for himself, but I would not look at them. He had obviously been under a great deal of pressure about his writing skills and he needed a break. Also, I intended to stimulate him so much intellectually that by the time he was allowed to write he would be bursting to share it on paper.

The Center closed for the first time in October of that year and we became a family school. Shirley, Earline, and all our children moved to the farm. We bought Hal and Julie first-grade math books, and Shirley's dad outlined a sixth-grade math curriculum for use with Craig. A tape recorder was made available to Craig, and sometimes he was asked to give on tape a reaction to some excursion we had taken. We took trips to the beach, the old train station, the cattle barn, and the Space Center.

School as a discipline was very informal. We let the children find us when they wanted to do school work. Only if a child was trying to cover too much material at once did we interfere with his work. On Christmas Eve of that year, Craig and Julie both asked for help with lessons. We enrolled Craig in a weekly judo class so he would have some contact with other boys his age. He also went weekly to one of the parks to study guitar with John.

The rest of the time we learned to work cattle, care for pigs and chickens, cut firewood, and plant a garden. The adults were as inexperienced at solving farm problems as the children were, so whenever one arose, each child's suggestion was considered as a possible solution.

In the spring Shirley, Karen, and Leavy reopened the Children's Center in a house in Nashville. Some days all our children went there. Other times we stayed at the farm. Shirley continued to live at the farm and drive the hundred miles each day to run the Center, and if something neat was going on in town, we went with her.

Each of the children progressed rapidly through the academic subjects. The most noticeable effect of that year of "non-school" was the amount of confidence Craig gained. He changed from a timid boy to a semi-aggressive young man. Also, before the year was over he could write a very legible short story. It wasn't easy for him, but he was willing to work at it until sentence structure, verb form, spelling, and punctuation were all correct. The most important element of his growth was that he knew he could do the work.

Hal was reading primers at the beginning of the year. Before it was over he was reading on the fourth-grade level. The most prestigious private elementary school in town, known for its academic excellence, tested him for entry into the second grade.

He was offered a slot.

He romped right through the math workbook and pushed himself to learn to write cursively. Although we were all excited about the growth we had seen in Craig and Hal, their daddies continued to be afraid of the legal status of our "un-school."

When the next school year began, Craig presented himself at his assigned school. He had a letter from me saying he had been in an ungraded school the previous year and was especially interested in horses and machinery. His new school sent a letter asking for a transfer of records. It was ignored, of course, because there were no records. Once back in public school, Craig's grades and confidence have continued to improve. Last year he made the highest score in the seventh grade of his school on the standardized literature exam.

I have already mentioned the altercation George and I had about entering Hal in public school. George was afraid that because he was a doctor someone would watch our family closely enough to realize the kids were not in school. He did not wish to have any publicized legal hassles with the public school system. The fact that we were operating under a legal charter and that Earline and I were both certified to teach in this state did not soothe him.

Hal went to school. After a brief period of testing he was placed in the highest reading group in his grade. He did, however, have some problems adjusting to the social structure of the class. He was startled that the children made fun of him when he took his green bear for "show-and-tell." He was puzzled that they didn't believe him when he talked about catching, saddling, and riding a horse by himself. He was impatient with their lack of discipline, and too proud of his own.

Once during the year the kids roughed him up in the classroom. When I found out about it I cried all night, but did not intervene. If second graders were capable of acting like that, things were bound to get worse, and he had better learn to fend for himself. Before the year was over, he had carved out a niche for himself with the children he really cared for.

This summer, as Julie neared the age of seven, she became excited about going to a real school. She could read satisfactorily, and was fast in math, but her printing was sloppy. I finally told her if she wanted to go to school she would have to do something about her handwriting—she did. She started the second grade on time. She, too, had problems with social adjustment. She did not see the humor in making fun of slow learners; instead she took up for them. She followed the teacher's directions with disgusting accuracy. At a conference on her recently, George and I learned she is in the top math and reading groups in her grade.

At the present time, Kelly is enrolled in a kindergarten class in the same school. However, at this time I do not intend to send her to the first grade. I am exploring the possibility of ballet lessons as a curriculum for her next year. Kelly is very bright, but at this time all she cares about reading are McDonald's and Baskin Robbins signs. She just is not interested in reading, writing, and arithmetic.

She is, however, extremely creative in art; music transforms her into a butterfly. She and I will spend next year exploring ways she can establish her identity other than making A's in reading or winning the hundred-yard dash. From experience I know she will learn to read at the same speed the children who are in the first grade will be reading. At the age of seven she will return to the class she is with now for the second grade.

Whenever we share with parents or educators the way we have dealt with school phobia, they are always astonished. I suppose the question asked most frequently is, "How did you get away with it?" meaning how did we trick the authorities. We didn't have to trick them because they never asked. The entire year Craig dropped out of public school, not one official ever contacted us to find out where he was. We have never made contact with other families doing a similar thing, but there must be some. Someone introduced a bill into the state legislature saying a school has to consist of more than one family and more than ten children. As far as I know, it didn't pass.

Even though our children are now enrolled in public school, we have not altered our lifestyle much. If George is free to go to the farm, we take the children out of school and go. We also spend time with the kids in the school setting. I spend one morning a week in

Julie's room in the language-arts center. Shirley has begun to spend one day a week in Kelly's room as a volunteer. Next week I am to go to Hal's class and cook a bicentennial meal with a group of students.

We have planned a trip to the ocean next month. The agenda is learning the metric system (I don't know it either), and studying the life of the sea. We try not to let school interfere with the children's education!

There are now several groups willing to lend support to parents who are dissatisfied with the public school system, and who are seeking a legal alternative. One of these is the National Association for the Legal Support of Alternative Schools. They can be contacted c/o Ed Nagel, P.O. Box 2823, Santa Fe, New Mexico, 87501.

One of their suggestions is particularly interesting to me. They encourage enrolling your child in an accredited alternative school in another state, and then having them approve a home study course. Periodically, records are sent to the school and credits are assigned for certain subjects. I think this idea is absolutely ingenious, and, though I'm satisfied with the school that serves my children now, it is comforting to know there is a legal way out.

Of course, this is only one of many possible solutions. Apprenticeships seem to have been long neglected. I am already compiling a mental list of farmers, craftsmen, mechanics, and professional people we know who might take on someone to sweep the floor. Another excellent source for keeping up with alternatives is the New Schools Exchange, Pettigrew, Arkansas, 72752. They cover many areas of child-rearing, including nutrition, parenting, and learning environments, and they publish an annual directory of alternative schools across the nation.

A caring parent can do something about an abhorrent school situation. The idea of education for all was originally to serve the people. I'm afraid that all too often, parents abdicate their responsibility for being the primary educators of the child to a system they know nothing about or feel powerless to change.

We as parents need to learn to bear our children's burdens, for they are heavy. Trying to rear an emotionally, socially, spiritually, intellectually, and physically healthy child in our present society demands great attention and support of parents.

Speaking the Truth to One Another in Love

A friend of Earline was speaking to me about her daughter once, and she said, "I just want her to grow up to be a decent human being."

My first impression was that it was a simple goal. However, the more I have thought about it, the more complicated "decent" has become. What is involved in being a decent human being? Webster defines decent as proper and fitting; not obscene; respectable; adequate; kind; and generous. I would add self-disciplined and honest.

By the restorative work of Jesus Christ in my life, I am becoming a decent human being. In my past lies rebellion, dishonesty, self-centeredness, arrogance, and the vestiges of destruction in the paths I walked. Some of the incidences from my childhood which were woven into the fabric of my old self are clear in my memory.

I was born during World War II, when sugar was a luxury. When I was four, Daddy brought home a box of assorted chocolate candy bars; they were probably the first I had ever seen. Mother gave me one, and it seemed the most wonderful thing I had ever tasted. I asked for another and Mother told me no.

When she went outside to hang clothes on the line, I climbed up on the cabinet and grabbed a Baby Ruth bar. I stuck it in my pocket and walked to a friend's house, sat down where I couldn't be seen from my house, and relished every bite of the candy.

Later in the day Mother missed the Baby Ruth. She asked me if I had taken it and I said that I had not. When my brother, Al, came home she asked him if he had eaten it. No, he hadn't. Daddy came in from work and she inquired if he had taken it. He didn't know anything about it.

Then she explained to me that stealing and lying were wrong, and paddled me with a butter paddle. I was angry with myself for getting caught, and resolved to cover my tracks better if ever I got in that situation again.

Last weekend at the farm Kelly was dressing in my bedroom when she told Shirley, "I know where Mother hides her candy. I could eat it, but I haven't because it would make her feel bad." Booth knows where I keep my candy, too. That one candy bar has been in my bookcase for three months. Why hasn't someone eaten it?

Probably because they, like Kelly, know it would make me feel bad. It is only a grocery-store candy bar; it could easily be replaced. They could rationalize that if I wanted it, I would have eaten it by now. Still, they don't bother it. There are several reasons for this.

First, if someone gave them candy and they wanted to save it, they know it would be where they put it when they came back for it. We respect their right of personal ownership; we expect them to respect ours. Secondly, their appetite for sweets is regularly overfed. The third reason is that if they took the candy without asking, I would punish them.

In teaching a child obedience and self-control, it is important to know how his mind works. Some four-year-olds can be given the information that "this is your candy bar and the other one is mine," and be expected to leave the other one alone. Others are not capable of functioning at that level of maturity. Shirley said she would not expect a child who had never been given candy to restrain himself from eating more. If she really did not want him to eat her candy, she would put it in a place where he could not find it.

I discussed with the extended family how they would have dealt with me when I was four and stole the Baby Ruth. George said he would probably do the same thing Mother did. Shirley said she would not have expected me to have self-control, so the candy would not have been where I could find it.

I think I had enough maturity at that time that if it had been explained to me that the other candy bars were for Al and Daddy, I would have left them alone. During that same time in my life there was only one piece of meat on the platter for each person in the family, and I don't think I usually asked for more than mine. I believe I even had an ability to feel protective of each person's right to his pork chop.

The most effective way to discipline is to prevent the wrong behavior. But since I did steal the candy bar and lie about it, had it been explained to me afterwards that my disobedience meant someone else would have to do without, I probably would have been truly sorry. Had my supper been withheld, I believe my attitude and behavior would have been corrected.

By the age of six, I had a real fear of the rod—I just did not like to be spanked. In the first grade, I sharpened a crayon in the pencil sharpener one day. When the teacher discovered the shavings she said, "Who sharpened a crayon in the pencil sharpener?"

I could tell she was angry, and since no one had told me not to sharpen crayons, I did not confess. I was spanked enough for things done on purpose, and I did not want to also be punished for things done accidentally.

I had a vague feeling at the time that not coming forward with the truth was the same thing as lying. Over the years, the guilt of withholding the truth in various situations became so acute that I began to fantasize that I didn't know the difference between the true and the untrue. Eventually, I sometimes didn't know.

One day in the second grade, I cheated on a spelling test. I wrote the words in the back of a workbook and copied one or two of them during the test. Tommy, who sat across the table from me, told on me. I denied it. Mrs. Moser was a wonderful teacher and I adored her. We both knew I had copied those words, but she chose to believe me. I don't think I ever cheated again in my whole school experience. (I did, however, make Tommy's life miserable for several years.)

When I was eleven, an incident happened which blocked my conscience from feeling guilty about lying. Linda, a friend, invited me to go home with her after school the next day and play. She said her mother would take me home at suppertime. I asked Mother and she said I could go.

The next afternoon Linda's mother was ill, and they asked me to come some other time. I had missed my ride home, so I walked to my aunt's house and tried to call Mother to tell her what had happened. I missed her at work and she wasn't home yet, so I walked home.

Meanwhile, Mother had discovered I wasn't at Linda's house, and had become frightened when she couldn't locate me. I was walking as fast as I could because it was twilight, and I was afraid of the dark and of Mother.

When I got home, I explained that I had gone to my aunt's and tried to call her so she would not worry about me. I had also hoped to get a ride home, but my aunt was at work.

I needed to be comforted, but it didn't work out that way. Mother had feared for my safety and by the time I got home she was very upset. I suppose she spanked me in a rage born of fear.

Several days later, I heard her gasp as I passed naked in front of her, and she noticed my bottom was bruised from the beating. Although she said she would never spank me again, it was not just my bottom that was injured. I had tried to be a responsible person acting as wisely as I knew how in a scary situation, and she had not believed me.

From then on, a lie became as good as the truth for me. While I basically wanted to be a good girl, if I messed up I didn't hesitate to lie about it. As I grew through my teens and early adult life, my dishonesty mushroomed and my whole life became a fabric of lies.

About the time I decided to quit pretending to be what I wasn't, and hiding what I was, I met George. He was the first man I ventured to be truthful with. Probably the reason I ever married him was because when he asked me really scary questions and I told him the truth, he didn't condemn me. This is not to say I was always honest with him; there were a lot of questions he didn't know to ask. There were also times when he knew to ask, but I was sure he would reject me if I told him the truth, so I lied.

Only through George's mercy and longsuffering, along with the support of a Christian community, have I begun to be a truthful person. For years George has overlooked many painful incidents with gentleness and grace because he wanted me to learn I would not be rejected if I told the truth.

Other family members have forgiven me when I have lied, and have given me positive verbal approval for the truth, even when they didn't like the answer. Although the entire family has had ample

SPEAKING THE TRUTH TO ONE ANOTHER IN LOVE

evidence to label me a liar, they have chosen instead to forgive me and expect me to tell the truth.

Had they chosen to expect me to lie, I would probably still be lying. Instead, their faith in me has inspired me to strive for a pure heart. That means I avoid having a hidden agenda. If I say I'm going someplace, I'm not also planning to make a stop they wouldn't approve of. If I say I will do something at a certain time, I don't have a previous conflicting commitment. I have moved beyond telling the truth just when asked, to keeping my word when I give it. This is a revolutionary development at our house.

There are several observations from my past which I hope make me a better parent. The rod did not beat the devil out of me. My fear of the rod probably let the devil in. The spankings not only did not bring me under authority, they increased my contempt for it. I feared power, but I did not respect it or submit to it. Like the story of the little boy who was brought in for discipline and told to sit down, I was standing up inside.

For my mother's sake I need to interject here that I think she disciplined me with the best of intention, and from where I stand now I would prefer all those spankings to no correction at all. I was so frequently in trouble that I knew she cared about me. I have a great love for her and always have had. Her discipline was not just negative; she also nurtured me. She read to me, taught me poems and Bible verses, took me to parades and movies, and regularly prayed with me and for me.

Although I have described myself as being pretty awful, most of my external behavior was acceptable or even admirable. Many goals I set and achieved were an attempt to gain her approval and affection; she freely gave both. This examination of how I came to be a chronic liar is very painful for me to write, and I'm sure it will be equally painful for her to read. This is an area of my life which witnesses to the redemptive power of Christ, and I believe there are many people with similar problems who need to know His power is available.

Some time ago, an incident happened at the farm which really impressed on me how easy it is to push a child into a corner by not believing him. Earline and I were in the kitchen when Hal, Julie, and Kelly came in arguing. Julie was crying and when she told me what had happened, I sent her and Kelly out. When Hal gave me his version of the story, I told him I thought he was lying and I pressured him until he started crying.

When he left the room, Earline calmly told me I might have missed something in the situation. She pointed out that Julie was upset because Hal had hurt her feelings. When I had talked with Hal, I had not mentioned he had hurt her feelings, but rather was hung up on the fact that he didn't tell the same story she did.

Earline said that whenever you ask a child what happened, you must accept the child's answer as the truth. She emphasized that I could choose not to ask, but if I did ask, my good relationship with the child demanded that I believe him. Hal knew he had done something to Julie he shouldn't have done. That's the reason it was hard for him to talk about it.

As I have grown into the security of believing it is okay to tell the truth, I understand more clearly what Earline was teaching me. We become what those people whom we love think we are. When the extended family took the position of believing and accepting me, no matter what I told them, my fear was gone. Once I was secure in their love, I wanted to be what they believed me to be. I accepted the responsibility for ordering my life in order to always be comfortable telling the truth.

We must expect our children to be truthful. We must also be careful to be truthful with them. In my own experience, my first attempts at a really pure relationship were with my children. At the time Hal and Julie were born, I was going through a stage of new spiritual awareness. I was just discovering that God has given us victory over the forces of darkness through the blood of Jesus.

At that point, all of my relationships with other people—even George—were hopelessly entangled in a net of deceit. I didn't then have the courage or the support to begin to walk a new life, but I knew there was a different way to relate to people than the way I had been living.

As I began to communicate with the children, I told them all the truth I knew. When they were babies in my arms, I told them things no one else knew but God and I. As they grew older and began to converse with me, I tried carefully to give them the facts as I understood them. Since they had no past experiences with me, there was no need to guard what I told them in order to cover my tracks.

Because learning to be honest has been such a personal struggle, and since my relationship with my children has been such a positive experience, I am acutely aware of the many ways parents lie to their children.

Have you ever heard a parent say to a small child "You are so bad!" Something that irritates me even more is to hear a parent say to a five-year-old child, "If you're not good, that policeman is going to get you."

What the parent really is saying to the child is, "I don't care enough about you to expend the energy to discipline you. You are embarrassing me by your behavior, and I wish you'd stop." Believe me, a five-year-old understands all the parent is really saying.

He also feels an anxiety toward the policeman because he's not sure the policeman won't get him, and he doesn't know what "get him" means. That child is probably also threatened with doctors, preachers, salesladies, and bus drivers. Probably none of those people ever correct him.

By the time that five-year-old is fifteen, he has learned that his parents don't like him enough to discipline him, and the many authority figures he has been threatened with are not going to discipline him either. The fear with which he has viewed these authority figures turns to disdain, then hatred. He begins to shoplift, or do something else which is socially unacceptable, hoping someone will catch him and give him some attention.

His parents choose to ignore the fact that he has clothes they did not buy or cannot account for. If he does get picked up in the act of stealing and put in jail, he finally gets some attention. His parents show up at the jail mumbling something about the fact that they never could do anything with him. They are in a furor because his behavior has embarrassed them. They probably also remind him that they told him if he wasn't good, the police were going to get him. They grudgingly take off from work to go to court with their child. If it is a first offense, the kid gets a suspended sentence and a long lecture from his parents about how they don't understand how he could do this to them. This teenager's heart is crying out through his behavior, *see me, hear me, stop me, care about me!*

What lessons can be drawn from this incident? Any parent of a preschool child who does not discipline and control that child is too self-centered to be a parent. However, if the parent could foresee that the child would one day find a way to get his undivided attention through severe embarrassment, he might take the trouble to control the child at the age of five.

It is a serious offense for a parent to lie to a child by threatening him with some ominous authority. It is serious not only because a lie is morally wrong, but also because it suggests the parent does not love the child. The lie is only the symptom; the parent's self-love is the disease.

Not only is speaking the truth important, but living the truth is essential if parents are to maintain an honest relationship with their children. We have an acquaintance who frequently drinks bourbon. This man has a twelve-year-old son who has been asking if he could taste his father's drink since he was a toddler. Recently, we were with that family and some of the adults were having wine with their meal. The boy asked me if he could have a taste of wine and I told him to check with his dad. His father reacted with a look that said, "You know you are not old enough to enjoy something this good," shaking his head no.

If that kid hasn't figured out by now where his father keeps his wine and liquor, and how to sneak some of it, he's not as smart as I think he is. His father has made a really big deal out of a basic issue. The boy probably has many unrealistic fantasies linking alcohol to manhood. Several years from now when the son comes home stoned on dope, the father will probably be very pious and puzzled.

Many Christians do not believe drinking is consistent with their Christian convictions and testimony. The point I want to make is not whether drinking is right or wrong for the Christian, but the importance of living the truth before children by being consistent. I believe that parents who drink alcoholic beverages ought to be honest enough to let their children sample them.

I had a friend in high school whose mother smoked in the maid's bathroom for years. The rest of the time she acted like smoking was some evil thing. Even after her daughter began to smoke in front of her, she didn't admit that she herself smoked. Anytime a parent lies to a child either verbally or through actions, the dishonesty is only a symptom. Beneath that symptom is usually a gangrenous disease.

IV
LOVE HOPES ALL THINGS

By now, some will think this book is fiction rather than an autobiography because of the sheer energy required to parent in the way this book suggests. This final section has a theme of *hope*.

Nearly all parents are dealing with some undesirable behavior in their child. There is a chapter in this section which offers suggestions and encouragement for erasing those habits.

The *Supermom* chapter shows you can make many mistakes and still get good results if your intent is right.

A chapter has been written upon request which deals with the kind of maturity levels at which our children function. Some of you won't believe it; others will be too shy to implement it; for some it will be a needed goal.

The final chapter attempts to lead parents who are seeking a new relationship with their children from havoc to heaven. It is a "how to do it" chapter.

Behaviors You Can Do Without

I have an acquaintance who never mentions her youngest child without adding, "He's a holy terror." Before I became a mother, a statement like that conjured up a fantasy of a cute little *Dennis the Menace* type boy. I usually felt a slight compassion for the poor bedraggled mother.

My feeling now is that "He's a holy terror" is a prophecy. For some time psychologists have taught about "self-fulfilling prophecy," the process by which a child becomes what he perceives himself to be. Earline told me that one time a mother introduced her five-year-old son by saying, "Mrs. Kendall, this is Dennis—Dennis the Menace." Earline said that child could hardly sit down in a chair without the leg falling off.

I don't understand the whole concept, but there must be something strange going on in the mind of any parent who continually announces his child is out of control. One factor may be that the parent doesn't like the child.

The first time I ever mentioned to my mother that I thought a particular mother didn't like her child, she came unglued. She was really angry at me for even suggesting that such a condition could exist.

I explained to her that most parents seem to like their children when they are babies. However, there seems to be a transition age, usually when the child begins to assert himself as an individual, when things sometimes change. It appears that what was enjoyment of the child may become tolerance of the child.

You don't have to be a psychologist to observe this. Last Wednesday morning Kelly, Booth, and I went to the local library for story hour. The children usually sit in the middle of the rug and most of the parents sit in folding chairs at the back of the room. There was a new child among the group last week, a little boy about five. I noticed him when we first went in because he was running around the room yelling. Although the children usually move around until the librarian sits down, he was unusually boisterous.

As the children sat down he continued to be disruptive. The storyteller asked him twice to be quiet; the third time she told him he would be sent upstairs if he didn't hush. If his mother was in the room, she didn't move.

I didn't intend to say anything to him, but as I crept past him to tell Booth I was going upstairs, he screamed in my ear. I looked him right in the eyeball and said, "Would you please be quiet?" He was startled, but shook his head yes. I said, "Thank you—you were disturbing the other children."

Since I had taken it upon myself to correct him, I didn't go upstairs. Twice he looked back to see if I was there. I was looking straight at him. He kept himself together the rest of the hour.

My immediate reaction had been to be angry with the child. After I thought about it I was angry with the mother instead. I believe parents who allow their children to develop patterns of anti-social behavior must not like them. There is no other reason I can think of why they allow the child to be disruptive. The natural result whenever a child or an adult is rebellious and disruptive in our society is for some *authority* to restrain him.

It is not my plan to personally discipline all the children in the world. I know that beneficial discipline cannot really begin until a child trusts me. Until he has enough experience with me to see I am interested in him, I can only temporarily change his behavior. A child has to know I intend to help him meet his spiritual, physical, social, intellectual, and emotional needs before he can really trust me. Once we have established that trust through shared experiences, he begins to acquire self-discipline. He has seen for himself that when we do things a certain way, his needs are fulfilled. Therefore, he begins to choose to do them that way, even if I'm not around.

Once a week we set aside a day to run errands. If we have had a long stay at the farm, there may be fifteen stops on my list. The children know from experience that before the day is over, we will make at least one stop especially for them. We might stop for twenty minutes at a favorite playground, or go to the ice-cream store, or stop by McDonald's for lunch.

Before we leave the house everyone goes to the bathroom. Booth always declares she doesn't have to but I take her anyway. After a bathroom stop, everyone passes through the kitchen for a drink of water. I offer only water when we are going somewhere because most other drinks make them thirsty.

With immediate physical needs met and the promise of a special kid stop, we begin our day. I usually don't play the radio when the children are in the car because riding is such a good time for communicating. I especially encourage the children to look for and share unusual sights. We slow down for construction projects, landing planes, new billboards, and beautiful landscapes.

I'm not afraid to take my children in any store. If I say, "don't touch," they usually don't touch. Each child is allowed one warning if he starts picking things up in a store. After that, he goes to the car. If for any reason he pitches a temper tantrum, we leave the store and go home. While this does not seem completely fair to the other children, it sure does encourage them to look after each other. They watch Booth closer than I do when we are shopping. One day in a clothing store Booth grabbed something and Hal immediately offered to take her to the car. I let him.

If we have to take the culprit home, he is put down for quiet time without lunch. Then I try to fix something special for the other children. If the behavior was particularly obnoxious, that child gets left at home the next time we go on a similar outing. We explain carefully that we don't intend to take him until he thinks he can keep himself together.

Before Shirley explained it to me I used to leave the kids in the car if I would only be a minute and if I could see them from inside. She pointed out that the process of getting in and out of the car releases energy. She also mentioned that the children were not going to learn a great deal about buying a stamp or leaving a coat at the dry cleaners from inside the car. Now, whenever I stop we all get out.

Yesterday, we stopped at a small shopping center and Kelly wanted to run. The sidewalk was clear both ways so I told her she could run to the end and back, but not to get off the sidewalk. Julie and Booth took off after her. In a minute all three were back. They had found a pet store with puppies in the window. We went down to the store and talked with the manager about the pups. He said they were Chows and told us a little about their care.

When we left the store, I began running and all four of us got some exercise. After two more quick stops we went to a drive-in market for drinks. Usually, if I'm thirsty, they are thirsty. If I need to find a bathroom, they do too. When I'm hungry, they are ready to eat. When shopping alone I try to put these stops off as long as possible, but when the children are with me I listen to my body.

This sensitivity to their needs has had an interesting effect. They almost never mention hunger or thirst. I stopped by a bathroom the other day and Kelly almost ran over me getting inside. She had not mentioned she needed to go. If it is one-thirty before I notice I'm hungry, they have not mentioned lunch. They are so sure lunch will be something special when we get around to it that they just wait and see. I have heard five-year-olds say they get a headache when they get too hungry. I always wonder who taught them that.

A lot of parents associate having enough to eat at the right time with personal security. We seem to have many people in our Western culture who eat by the clock in order to feel secure. When it's time to eat lunch, they eat whether they are hungry or not.

Kids are not hung up with food and security being the same thing. They listen to their bodies. If they aren't hungry, they won't eat unless some adult forces them to. When they realize eating is a big deal for the adults, they sometimes use that as a weapon against their parents. If they are angry about something, they just won't eat. This supposedly punishes the parents.

What Booth has eaten the last three days wouldn't fill two cups. I figure she is either caught up on her eating, is getting ill, or is trying to find out if she can decide to eat or not. She can. Around this house you can eat or not eat. If you plan to eat you had better show up when

BEHAVIORS YOU CAN DO WITHOUT

supper is on the table. I don't allow a child who skips a meal to pop into the kitchen and eat cookies between meals. He can have cookies after he eats the next meal.

Most four-year-olds are pokey. They either can't or won't move as fast as they did when they were three. I guess they are just absorbed in what they are doing. Whenever I'm serving meals and there is a child of four in the house, I try to give him the fifteen-minutes-till-supper warning call. This gives him a chance to finish what he is doing.

Then, as the meal is served, I make sure he gets the word. If he doesn't show up by the time everyone else finishes, I throw his meal out. Sometimes it takes three times before he figures out he is expected to function at meals like everyone else.

We have defined clearly for the children what we expect from them at mealtime. We don't allow the children to run around the house with food in their hands. (I don't like to vacuum that much!) Sometimes we move the little table into their room and feed them breakfast while they watch cartoons, but we *always* eat at the table.

Once we all get to the table the children are expected to sit in their own chairs, speak in a normal voice, and not dominate mealtime conversation. We often have fourteen people around the table at the farm. The children are interspersed among the adults so they can be helped when necessary. They are included in the conversation but are not allowed to steal the show.

If a child leaves the table even once, I clear his plate. The exception is if he has asked to be excused and says he will be right back. After a child takes his plate to the kitchen, he is expected to stay away from the dining area until everyone else has finished. It really bothers me to eat at a table where children hang around the table whining and climbing on the chairs.

When the adults finish their meal, the children may come back to the table for dessert. If a child has been disruptive during mealtime, he misses dessert.

There are certain behaviors we don't tolerate at mealtime. Any child who misbehaves at meals receives only one warning. After that he is told to go to his room. Depending on the infraction, he may or may not be allowed to finish. The adult who sent him out and goes to his room to talk with him decides that.

We don't bring babies to the table during mealtime. Recently, a couple with a six-month-old baby was eating supper with us. When we gathered around the table the daddy had her on his shoulder. During the blessing she began to cry loudly. As soon as the "amen" was said, I took her from her daddy, told her we didn't allow crying at the Andrews table, and took her to another room. I can't think of any reason why a baby should come to the table during meals until he can sit in a highchair and nibble quietly on a cracker.

Pouting at the table is also out. Since we spend a lot of time teaching the children how to express themselves when they need to, and since I don't care whether they eat or not, all pouters are banned from the table. If they go to their rooms and put on happy dispositions, they can finish their meals if they are still there. If they are really hungry they manage to correct their attitudes fast.

My personal philosophy is that it takes three rounds to change any behavior pattern. Those three encounters are distressing for the child and agonizing for me. If I'm convinced a change needs to be made, I set my face like flint, notify all the other family members, and charge head-on into the battle.

When Shirley first came to live with us, Hal had me dancing a jig. He woke up at five-thirty every morning starving to death. Being a morning person anyway, I didn't really mind the early hour and rose at five to make sure breakfast was ready as soon as he cried.

Shirley is not a morning person and she thought five was a ridiculous hour to serve breakfast. She didn't say anything for about three months—she just watched. Then one morning she got up and changed Hal, told him he could have breakfast when he quit crying, and shut the door to his room. You could have knocked either Hal or me over with a feather.

It is only fair to Shirley to point out that by now Hal was twenty months old, with a shape similar to a beach ball. She figured the chances of him starving to death between five-thirty and seven were very slim. The next morning we went through the same routine. He was very angry by now and made a real fuss. The instant he quit crying long enough to breathe, Shirley opened the door and told him since he was through crying, he could eat. He blew it, and started crying again, and it was about fifteen more minutes before he stopped.

That night as we put him to bed, Shirley put a toy at the foot of his crib and told him he could play with it when he woke up. She assured him we would be in to get him when breakfast was ready.

It worked! The next morning the only noise from his room was the jingle of the bell on his toy. Shirley told him how nice he had been as she got him ready for breakfast.

This may sound like an unnessarily harsh way of dealing with a baby. In our household it has been an important aid in socializing the children. Julie, Kelly, and Booth learned this same lesson by the time they were a year old. After the episode with Hal, we didn't pick up a baby who was crying just because he wanted to eat right then. We always tried to offer food before he cried for it. If he got hungry early, we prepared the food but we didn't pick him up until he was quiet. We establish early that we are really happy to have a baby in the house, but the baby is not the only person there.

When Booth was born the entire family turned out. The day she and I came home from the hospital, Robert from New York, Susan—a college student, James and Walter—our two teen-aged foster sons, Linda, Shirley, our other three children, and George were there to greet us. I stayed in my room most of the first two weeks so I have no idea where all those people were sleeping.

In addition, we had daily visits from morning until midnight. We had a Children's Center board meeting in my den when she was ten days old.

I love a baby. I'd have one or two a year if we could afford to buy shoes for them. I sleep with one ear and both eyes open whenever there is a baby in the house. Since our household is so complicated, I reserved the right to feed Booth when she first came home. I felt like she and I needed that time to get acquainted. She needed to be aware of the confidence I had in caring for her.

Everyone in the house was dying to hold her. I let the children have the first turn. I just laid her in the middle of the bed and let them gather around and feel her. Then each child held her in his lap. Different people took turns diapering or bathing her. After she was full and had on dry pants, I let anyone who wanted to hold her have a turn.

We have a rule at our house that a baby should only be put to bed once. Even when we were bungling along as new parents we never picked up a child who had just been put down to nap.

I confess I spent a lot of time wondering if that was the right choice. I'd check to see if the diaper was wet. Sometimes from the volume of noise I'd be sure a pin had come loose and stuck the baby in the stomach, but that was never the case. After a pat on the back and a reassuring word, I'd get my courage up and leave him in the bed.

Even though the entire family understood this was our policy about bedtime, I had a hard time enforcing it with Booth. Someone was constantly sneaking in to pick her up when they thought I was napping. One night when she had been fed, burped, diapered, held, and put to bed, she began to cry. I slipped into her room unseen through a back hallway, and sat down in a rocker next to her bed. In the following twenty minutes, five different people quietly opened the door to come to her rescue. I just grinned and shook my finger at each of them.

At age three, Booth still gets put to bed just once. She has a lot of energy and unless she has a great deal of exercise every day, she has trouble falling asleep at night. Nevertheless, she is taken to the potty, given a drink, and put to bed at eight-thirty just like the other children. I usually give her a book, or puzzle, or a dolly and tell her to lie down when she is through playing with them.

We send them all to the bathroom, give them a glass of water to set beside their bed, let them select a favorite toy, then tuck them in and expect them to stay there until morning. Any child who fails to cooperate willingly is put to bed thirty minutes earlier the next night.

We don't make any attempt to be quiet when the children are asleep. In the first place there are too many of us. The first two weeks after Booth was born, she slept in a bedroom beside the den so I could tend her without having to climb the stairs. That meant everyone who came to visit passed by her door. It also meant that whenever the television or stereo was on she could hear them. Each of our babies has been treated this way. We have had several gatherings in the apartment that went on for hours after they were in bed, and they slept through it all.

We have a routine the children follow when they wake up in the morning. I know families whose kids have been up, eaten a bowl of cereal, and scattered all over the neighborhood before the parents wake up. That would scare me to death.

Even though I'm up very early in the morning, I still don't intend to entertain a child who can't think of anything to do. When we put Booth to bed we tell her that unless she needs to "tinkle" she is to stay in bed until we come get her in the morning. The older children don't have to stay in bed, but they are expected to entertain themselves quietly in their rooms until we call them for breakfast. Any child who is loud enough to be heard before we call them is either read the riot act or is asked to stay in his room for an extra period of time.

Hal wakes up early. He usually bathes and dresses and then reads until we call him. I opened Julie's door the other morning and she was sitting dressed at the typewriter. She grinned and said she was writing a song and that I couldn't see it yet. This early morning quiet time has become as valuable to them as it is to me.

In this discussion of changing behaviors I have yet to mention spanking. I do sometimes spank one of the children. It is always the last choice for modifying behavior.

The first choice is defining before each activity what the positive choices are—what behaviors we consider appropriate. We not only define the choices, but also ask the children to repeat them to us so we know they understand. If a child then chooses to misbehave, we remove him immediately from the situation.

There are two reasons for this. First, we do not intend to shame or label the child in front of other people. We don't want him to be embarrassed to go back into the situation once his behavior is changed.

The second reason we remove him is that we have such a warm fellowship within the family that separation from the group feels like punishment to the child. Our children already have a personal interest in perpetuating group activities. We reserved a skating arena and took the family skating yesterday, and Hal pestered us to all join hands and skate together. When we are at the farm, the children regularly come up with suggested activities for the entire family. They have a respected place in the group and are eager to conduct themselves in such a way that they are allowed to participate.

The real secret of our approach to discipline is that the children receive so much affection and approval from individual family members that they easily internalize self-discipline. They are not petted, but they are given the same kind of respect and consideration the adults receive.

Not many people have access to a community fellowship for their children, but there are many ways parents can give positive reinforcement. A double-dip ice cream cone served with the comment, "I really appreciate your patience with me while we ran all those errands today. I think I'd like to have you along next time I shop," can go a long way toward encouraging the child to control himself. "Thanks for remembering to bring your dirty clothes to the laundry room—that really helps me," causes a child to glow inside. Look for ways to let the child know you *feel good* when he responds properly.

I talked with a father the other day who trains his children by spanking them regularly. He said he spanks them the first time they don't do what he told them to do. He spends a lot of time nurturing them, making sure they know what to do and why they are to do it.

We agreed that there are two reasons his way works for him and our way works for us. We consistently deal with the behavior before it occurs or immediately after we get the first wrong response. Neither of us nag the children. Neither of us issues threats we don't intend to carry out. Depending on the situation and the child's age, we sometimes give one reminder, or warning. After that, the children know they will be punished.

The second similarity between us is the amount of time we are willing to spend with our children training them. Our conversations with them are not limited to yelling over our shoulders in a department store to "put that down." We perceive our roles as parents as one of great responsibility. We both have received the benefits of loving, obedient children.

The Supermom Myth

I just read this book and it sounds pretty good. In fact, it makes me feel like Supermom. I will now use this pen to pop that bubble.

Shirley is able to see a child's behavior developing, project in her mind what that behavior is going to look like when the child is seven instead of eighteen months old, and then act to encourage or curb the pattern depending on whether or not it is something we want the kids to do as they get older.

On the other hand, I have trouble seeing past the immediate behavior and thinking it is imaginative or funny. There have been times when I have agreed intellectually to discipline a behavior when emotionally I really didn't want to. This always hurts me.

Actually, Supermom is a pretty average person who by God's grace walks most of the time in her gifts instead of her weaknesses.

I know most of my strengths. I have a great love of life, a real joy in filling every day with creative activity. I am comfortable in large groups of people, and have a God-given gift to organize tasks and make people feel at home. I care very little for material possessions and thus can share food, shelter, and pocket change with ease. It is difficult for me to give up hope on any person who is down. Anyone I have ever loved has a protected place in my heart.

I also confess to being very aware of my weaknesses. I often agree to do things I really don't have the time or inclination to do. I function well in crowds, but require a large amount of private time. I usually get up at five every morning to read and pray, and get pretty uptight if anyone tugs at me before seven. Usually an hour of quiet time or napping in the afternoon is also required to maintain my sunny disposition.

While I am gifted at creating and initiating projects, I am a poor finisher. My family has prayed with me about this and are faithful to encourage me to complete a task once it is begun. They have contributed hours of reinforcement during the writing of this book. They have read and re-read it, edited, suggested, prayed about it, shared it with others, and have many times stepped into my role as mother and housewife in order to free me to work. They have been very patient with me about typing for three months on the dining room table.

I am just past being a "screamer." Until a year ago, I often got nervous around suppertime and would find myself being verbally abusive with the children. Instead of listening to them, I just screamed orders. After much discussion and prayer with the group, I realized much of the problem was scheduling. I would take on so many projects for the day that I was always behind. By suppertime I was exhausted and pressured to catch up and have supper ready on time.

I have prayed about yelling because I felt a lot of guilt about coming down on the kids. After praying for "a gentle and quiet spirit, wisdom, purity of purpose, and guidance for each day's activities," I am much more pleasant to be with most of the time. On days when I'm particularly sensitive to noise or annoyed by some behavior, I speak as honestly as I can about it to the children.

The most important confession I must make is that my children are not perfect. There are very few times when all four children are functioning as well as we would like them to. Shirley will say, "We need to watch Kelly and see that she does what she's told to do." At that point, the entire family begins to focus on improving that behavior. Hal's behavior is rarely bad, but sometimes we have to alter his attitude. Growth happens each day, and we constantly have to re-evaluate where each child is and what behaviors need to be reinforced.

Recently, I was having a lot of trouble being peaceful with Julie. She would ask a question and when I answered, she would push me about whether or not I had told her the truth. If I answered a question

THE SUPERMOM MYTH

someone else had asked, she would contradict me or raise some doubt about the answer. I began to feel negatively toward her and would yell at her or just send her away.

After intense prayer, I came to three conclusions. One, I must always be sure to answer her with all the truth I have. Secondly, I realized the reason I was angry with her was because my feelings were hurt when she doubted me. I determined to communicate to her that how she felt about me really mattered, and that when I tried to speak honestly and she doubted me, I felt hurt. Lastly, I decided we needed to spend some time doing creative things away from the other kids. Thankfully, those things were the solution to the problem, but every day brings new crises which require prayerful solutions.

I am not always gentle, quiet, wise, or functioning as a whole person. Some days it just gets lost completely. I may be annoyed with the children or some of the adults, or be physically exhausted; sometimes I just plain get depressed. Usually Shirley, Earline, Karen, or Linda will assume the role of mother and I can hide out and get myself together.

Other days the same thing which has disturbed me might be bothering the other adults, and we are all at emotional and functional lows. On those days the children are expected to work around us. We expect them to make allowances for our bad days, and they do this beautifully. Earline says it is not as devastating to the children to see us all at a low ebb as it would be if they were depending on just one parent who lost it.

Anyhow, on bad days the chores always seem to get done more promptly and efficiently. Hal, Julie, and Kelly pitch in and help Booth find her socks and get her coat, and voices are a little more hushed.

We plan ahead for bad days, so the children will have some positive alternatives. About four times a year we sort toys. We put every single toy in one room and get the puzzle pieces, blocks, and tinker toys back in the proper boxes. We then take four or five boxes and put a variety of tasks in it—small-muscle, large-muscle, games, role-playing, and art materials.

We always do this job on days when we feel especially good so the boxes will be imaginative and the activities well rounded. Next we put all but one box in the top of the closet. Then on a day when

Shirley or I, or whoever is mother, is at a low ebb, we pull out a new box for the kids to explore.

We also send the kids one or two at a time on errands with various people who drop by and would be glad to have a small companion for a while.

With the support of the extended family, some days which are especially low for me become times of special sharing with the children individually. One day before the Lord delivered me from regular migraine headaches I stayed in bed all day. Shirley ran the house and dealt with the children, but as my head cleared I let them come into the room one at a time and share a story or just quiet conversation. George and I have always had a policy not to let a child sleep in the bed with us, so just getting to spend a few minutes on that big waterbed, cuddled up against Mother, was a real treat to them.

There are days when I fall apart and there is no one else around to take up the slack. On those days I begin by telling the children what the problem is—"I woke up with a headache," or "I feel sad so I may not act very nice." Then I give them as many positive choices for things to do as possible such as, "There's a new box of library books in the front closet," "I'll get the Fisher-Price garage and village down and you can play with that in your room;" "You may fix your lunch and go on a picnic," or " 'Electric Company' will be on in an hour." They know I'll be in my room if they need me. They have never failed to come through when I needed them.

Last Monday Shirley left to go to Chattanooga and work for Christmas money. Shirley has been with us the last six Christmases, and when she left I felt a little blue—not ugly, just very quiet. In a while Julie handed me this note: "Dear Mom, if you are sad because Shirley is gone I am sorry. Love, Julie."

We almost blew it with Julie. She was a toddler when Shirley and I were formulating our child-rearing philosophy, and she often did not get the benefit of the doubt. I remember particularly that she used to lose her shoes. We would be getting ready to go somewhere and she would start crying while she looked for her shoes. Shirley would yell at her to hurry up and she would cry harder.

It took us a long time to figure out she was afraid we would leave her; she needed assurance that we wouldn't. By training her to put her shoes in the same place so she could find them, she became worried less often.

One of the residual behaviors from this mishandling of Julie is what Shirley calls "parroting." She gets all the facts in her head as to what we are doing and then asks me if that's what we're doing. I'll start toward her school and she'll say, "Are we going to my school first?" Obviously we are, because I go a different way to take Hal first. She does this because she knows she'll get an affirmative answer from me. This means she and I still have not worked through all our problems.

It does not mean Julie is not okay. About three years ago it became apparent that being squeezed in between Hal and Kelly, plus our mishandling of her, had caused Julie to have a poor self-concept. For eighteen months we all worked on giving her positive reinforcement. She was given more opportunities to do things alone with me. Sometimes this meant someone else took the other three children and left her alone, and sometimes it meant I used my quiet time to share with her.

Linda and Susan seemed to especially enjoy her and they spent time with her. Sometimes she and I would get all dressed up and go out to eat with Daddy and her grandparents. We enrolled her in gymnastics and took special pains to see that she got there. After much prayer, attention, and time, Julie bloomed like a rose. Hallelujah!

Because she went through some emotional trauma when she was little that the other children didn't go through, she is especially sensitive to other peoples' feelings. When she handed me the note I just hugged her and said, "That's exactly what is wrong. Thank you."

Practical Results

It has become a trend in our urban, technological society to discriminate against the maturing of children. More and more, opportunities for them to make and live with their decisions are being eliminated. It appears we don't have a valid ritual for initiating our offspring into adulthood.

From birth to five years most children are left with caretakers who provide food, shelter, and some degree of safety. In most cases there is very little mental, physical, spiritual, or emotional stimulation. The children are usually stimulated socially because there are other kids there, and each child must establish and maintain a place in the social structure. Since many children are coming from homes where violence is perpetuated, however, the social interaction most preschoolers have could not be called positive.

We live in an apartment complex of middle-income families. There are probably seventy-five children here. The first dozen times any of our children went to the playground, someone offered to beat them up. At first, our kids didn't know how to react to that situation. After a year, they have carefully made a few friends. Most of those are children who at first threatened them, then found that it sure did feel nice to be respected because you are you, rather than for how many other kids you can bully.

I know several directors of day-care centers who are dedicated to the positive nurturing of little children. Those few encourage creative play and interact with the children in order to help establish values, but I know many others who believe if they feed the children, keep them clean, and give them a nap they have performed a valuable service.

At the age of five or six, children become students. Students are people who go to school most of the year to learn what other people think they need to know. What happens to them at school has very little to do with their desire, maturity level, or natural curiosity. The entire experience is totally out of their control. In school they are fed, sheltered, given some degree of safety, and given some mental, physical, spiritual, emotional, and social exposure.

I use the word exposure because if for any reason the child is not ready to learn today's lesson, then tomorrow he is behind and soon receives the label "failure." If the student complains to his parents about problems which arise at school, he is often told that these are the best, the easiest years of his life! Each year the number of deaths per thousand teen-agers by suicide increases.

At the tenth-grade level, our school system demands a remarkable thing of the student. It asks him to write down on paper what he wants to do the rest of his life. This is so the school will know whether the student should pursue a vocational or an academic course of study.

The student has literally been oppressed up to that grade level whenever he tried to actively participate in making decisions which affected him. For years, he has had his lunch handed to him in the cafeteria. What he ate, the maximum amount he could eat, and how much it cost has always been decided for him. He has had no opportunities for work experience—our state and federal laws see to that. If he has been very resourceful in mowing lawns or walking dogs in order to earn money, he cannot put it in the bank unless he wants to put it in a savings account which is co-signed by his parent.

The opportunities vary for assuming responsibility at home. Some students at the age of fourteen have never prepared a meal, never done the laundry, never mowed the yard, never repaired anything around the house, never even selected the clothes they wear.

One morning when I was a freshman in college, I was preparing breakfast for a friend who had spent the night with me. She wandered into the kitchen and asked if there was something she could do. I said, "Sure, butter the toast." She hesitated a moment, then asked me how to butter toast.

There was a time when parents paid a fee in order to apprentice their child to someone to learn a trade. It is probably true that those children didn't have much choice about their training, but at least they were prepared at the end of the apprenticeship to provide for themselves. Many of them used their vocation to support themselves while they studied for another position, but they were self-sufficient.

In our current situation, we put off the child's desire to care for himself until he is no longer interested in doing so. We train food service managers who have never cooked a meal, farmers who have never touched a cow, and psychiatrists who have no more experience with life than anyone else.

Most people know that what I have said is true. They are either satisfied with the system as it is, they have dropped out of society into their own trip, or they feel powerless to change things. I agree that parents have probably lost control of the machine, but unless they have wanted to, they have not lost control of what takes place within the home.

Before parents can transfer responsibility to their children a network of trust between the two must develop. How do you learn to trust a child? I quote Shirley. "You tell them what to do and you watch them. You teach them what to do and you watch them. You train them and you watch them. You tell them what to do and you leave them alone."

Since we have been developing shared responsibility and mutual trust with the children from birth, we allow them to engage in activities and tasks most people think are for adults only. They have as much freedom as they are able to cope with.

The activities the children engage in are divided into two areas. The first is responsibilities—those things we expect the children to do. The second is privileges—those things the children are allowed to do because they did what we expected them to do.

It is unwise to reverse that order. In the public school, every child is given the opportunity to take a course which teaches him how to drive a car. They can take this course because they have stayed alive for sixteen years. As far as I know, they are not expected to

PRACTICAL RESULTS

show *responsibility* in any other area before they receive the *privilege* of driving. That is not the way we do things at our house.

Throughout the book, I have mentioned areas of responsibility we expect the children to assume. For the benefit of those who missed it, I will restate some of the details. We expect each child who is at least three years old to be able to dress himself. After being told what the agenda is for the day, and what type of clothes are appropriate for the weather, each child selects his own outfit. Booth sometimes needs help with buttons or pullover shirts. We expect the other children to help her with those things. When they take their clothes off at night it is their job to either take them to the washing machine or put them up if they aren't soiled.

Each child has his own toys and his own space in which to store them. It is his job to pick up the toys after play and put them where they belong. If one child borrows another's toys, he must put them back in good shape. If he doesn't, we support the owner's right to refuse to lend his toys. That right is supported anyway, but the children rarely refuse to swap toys unless they are brand new.

On clean-up days, each child is responsible for cleaning his area to the best of his ability. We judge the results according to how much effort the child put into the job, and what his attitude is, rather than just by the outward appearance. If Booth and Hal spend the same amount of time cleaning their rooms, one would naturally expect Hal to get more done. We expect them to maintain enough order to find their belongings, even if it isn't clean-up day.

Each child happens to have a set of coupons to McDonald's and one to Baskin-Robbins. The other night, Shirley told them to get their McDonald's coupons and she would take them out to eat. Booth said, "I know where mine is," and in sixty seconds she showed up with it. They got the coupons four months ago and Booth has kept up with hers that long.

They are allowed to arrange their rooms any way they choose. Hal regularly moves the furniture in his room.

We expect the children to be responsible for each other. Hal, Julie, and Kelly are supposed to know where Booth is and to judge if she is in a safe place when they play outside. Booth is responsible to keep the other children in sight and to tell one of them if she is moving to another area or coming inside.

If the adults are away from the house and the children are inside, the oldest child there is responsible for the care of the others, who are expected to behave in such a way that they won't be any trouble to care for. There have been days at the farm when we were working outside through the lunch hour. We never stay away from the house very long if we can't see the house from where we are working, but if we can, we sometimes work nonstop.

In that event, the children are expected to fix their lunch and clean up after themselves. They are quite resourceful about planning menus and preparing meals. If we are still outside when quiet time comes, they are supposed to remind Booth to go to her room and then find something to do away from each other.

The adults in the family fold and sort the laundry, but the children can start the washer and dryer. Each child is responsible for picking up his clean clothes and putting them in the proper drawers. They also take out the trash, vacuum their rooms, clean their bathroom, remove their utensils from the table when they are through eating, and help clear the table. They are capable of loading and unloading the dishwasher without supervision, but it is not one of their regular chores.

The children have full responsibility for the care of the animals on the farm at this time. That includes dogs, cats, rabbits, chickens, and horses. Hal usually waters the chickens, Julie feeds them, and Booth and Kelly take turns carrying out the scrap bowl and gathering the eggs. About once a month they clean out the chicken house. Craig and Hal shovel and sweep the floor while the girls clean out the nests and put fresh hay in them.

Since domestic pets don't turn into food on the table, a child must be old enough to be responsible for a dog or a cat before he can have one. That includes noticing if the animal is injured or sick, and seeing that the pet is properly trained so it is not a nuisance.

The horses are Craig's special domain, and Hal is his apprentice. "Red Horse" belongs to Craig and Hal has a yearling named "Baby." Baby was born on the farm and her care and training have been strictly up to Craig and Hal, who have done an admirable job. She usually comes like a dog when you call her. They also catch, groom, saddle, and put up the horses anytime the family or visitors want to ride.

They also catch, groom, saddle, and put up the horses anytime the family or visitors want to ride.

When one of the children has shown himself to be a responsible person by doing his tasks faithfully, we are willing to let him tackle any piece of equipment or any task he is physically big enough to handle.

Being allowed to use machinery and tools is a privilege. It does not, however, require superior mental skills, and it isn't a valid badge of manhood. Craig and Hal are both allowed to bushhog and disc with the tractor. Julie is not quite big enough to handle the tractor, but she can use the Minimac chain saw.

Chain saws are dangerous; I have seen people in emergency rooms who have been injured by them. But I don't let her hold it unless she is on level ground, until I have checked to make sure there are no rocks or pieces of metal she might hit, and unless she is cutting no higher than her waist. Given those precautions, she has as good a chance as anyone for having a safe and satisfying experience.

I know it sounds like something out of *Tom Sawyer,* but Craig, Hal, and Julie compete to cut the yard. Our yard is about three acres and they use the tractor and a power mower to cut it. None of them has ever complained about doing it.

Last year we had a jeep-type vehicle on the farm which Hal and Craig both drove. Hal had to drive it standing up because he was too short to sit on the seat and see out. Even with that small handicap he could back it right up to the barn to load hay, or pull a stuck car out of the creek.

Learning to use and care for hand tools is another privilege available to the children. While Hal can put together something resembling a bird house, Booth is satisfied to hammer nails into soft wood. We have several shovels we bought at the Army surplus store which are just the right size for the children. They are also supervised while they learn to use saws, knives, hatchets, screwdrivers, and drills.

Being allowed to use a tool implies we think they are responsible enough to put them back in the proper places when they are through with them. They usually do, but if they forget, the privilege is withdrawn for a period of time.

I prefer to cook without the assistance of the children, so an invitation to help with a meal is considered a privilege. I'm not talking about fixing sandwiches—Hal or Julie frequently pack lunches for school or a picnic. The kind of cooking special to the children includes things such as cookies, biscuits, doughnuts, fritters, pancakes, or coffee cake. They also like to help with supper when there is meat to fry, salad to be chopped, and vegetables to be prepared.

Besides the educational aspects of learning to measure, following directions, and realizing why certain foods served together make a nutritious meal, the children receive the psychological benefit of being part of a whole. They get immediate reinforcement when we sit down to eat and George declares those are the best biscuits he ever ate.

Some of the trips we take with the children are a privilege. While they enjoy themselves most of the time when we travel, we sometimes plan outings just for them. The train trip to the Huntsville Space Center which I mentioned earlier is an example of such a trip. Although I enjoyed the trip, it was not something I would pick out just for myself.

Last summer, we took all five kids on an overnight camping trip. They were responsible for getting together the gear they thought they would need; they also participated in planning the menu, gathering the supplies, and setting up the campsite. They gathered firewood, dug a fire pit, laid the fire, chopped the vegetables for the stew, and took care of the clean-up chores. While the trip was a privilege, it came about only because they are able to function at a level of maturity which demonstrates they are responsible people.

As our children acquire new levels of responsibility, they are given more privileges. Many times the privileges are learning experiences which, once mastered, become new responsibilities. Once again more privileges are extended. Eventually, *responsibility* and *privilege* begin to overlap like ripples in a pond. Once that happens, the children have internalized much self-discipline and can be trusted to function as responsible people.

Train Up a Child in the Way

I believe man is created in the image of God. Every parent who has embraced a newborn infant has felt some awe at the miracle of that child, whether he professes to believe in God or not. While children have the capacity to commit acts which are truly wrong, they can also be trained to make choices which are truly right. It is our duty as parents to call forth God's likeness, to recognize, even to emulate it.

In Matthew 18, these words are recorded: "At that time the disciples came to Jesus, saying, 'Who then is greatest in the kingdom of heaven?' And He called a child to Himself and stood him in their midst, and said, 'Truly I say to you, unless you are converted and become like children, you shall not enter the kingdom of heaven. Whoever then humbles himself as this child, he is the greatest in the kingdom of heaven.' "

When I came upon that passage, sirens went off in my head. We usually parent by trying to change the child to be like us. Jesus said we must become like the child. I went to Webster for a definition of humble: 1. having or showing awareness of one's defects; modest. 2. lowly, unpretentious.

Are we as parents lowly and unpretentious before our children? Do we approach them with an attitude that we are imperfect? If so, then maybe we are ready to provide godly discipline for the child.

When Hal was born I became a "seeker of truth" on how to parent. That means I have been in the school of parenting nearly nine years. I have read books, journals, magazines, gone to workshops, seen

TRAINING UP A CHILD IN THE WAY

films, talked to experts, observed classrooms and day-care centers, volunteered as a parent, teacher, or aide, and prayed a great deal for the wisdom to raise my children in a godly way. This book is a diary of the way the Spirit has led me and the extended family in parenting.

Some parents who read this will have worked out another way of being a good parent—praise the Lord! There will be others who are doing something similar to what we are doing. The book will provide reinforcement and comfort to them. Still others will think our way is absolutely wrong. I pray that their anger might lead them to grow.

I address myself now to the seekers—the parents who really desire to be good parents, but don't know how. To those who want a way out, whose household is a disaster area because the children are in control, I offer a small light at the end of the tunnel.

In Col. 3:20 Paul wrote, "Children, obey your parents in all things; for this is well pleasing unto the Lord." If you have children who do not obey, you have a problem. However, unless their disobedience creates tension in you, you probably are not motivated to change the behavior. If you are in a state of tension with your child, and you care enough about him to go through the upheaval a change will bring, then I extend hope and these suggestions.

1. *Begin with hope*. Any parent can change a child's behavior. Read 1 Corinthians 13 and cling tenaciously to the phrase, "Now abideth faith, hope, love, these three; but the greatest of these is love." Those parents who are tapped into God as their power source have even more hope.

Cultivate faith. Every person has faith. It may not be a spiritual faith in a spiritual God. It may only be faith that if he turns his key, his car will start. In attempting to change a child's behavior, faith is the picture in your head of what the child will be like after he has changed. Exercise your imagination by creating situations in which the child reacts and interacts in an ideal way. Hold to the belief that he can be that kind of person.

Finally, *add love*. Love is the most important ingredient. An undisciplined child usually does not perceive that he is loved. As you work through the period of time it takes to bring the child under control, much love will be required from you, the parent.

In the initial phase of the change, the child will do some very unlovely things. When that happens, look again at that mental image of what he is becoming, and hang in there with love.

Some parents use the withdrawal of love to control a child, the way a child refuses to eat in order to control the parent. That is wrong because our love is supposed to be unconditional. It is possible to disapprove of the child's actions, and yet let him know you are loving him. One of the things he must know is that you love him. The parent needs to assume the attitude, "*You are,* therefore I love you."

2. *Pray that you will discern the true problem.* Lying is a symptom of a problem. Smoking dope is a symptom of a problem. Whining is a symptom of a problem. Although these symptoms can become problems, they initially are masks for rebellion, unbelief, and self-love. Parents often nag the symptom, thereby accentuating it, never realizing they are not dealing with what's really wrong.

3. *Develop a philosophy.* Once you have recognized that your child needs discipline, after you have put on the battle array of faith, hope, and love, and have prayed to discern the spiritual problem, then you need a philosophy to guide you through the process of change.

Recently, I asked a group of mothers if they would each share their philosophy of child-rearing. One mother gave a fairly complex answer, another knew some things she didn't want for her child, and another said she didn't know what a philosophy was.

For me, a philosophy is a framework within which to move. It is the game plan, the blueprint by which I plan to rear my children. By definition, my philosophy is "to rear my children to believe and to serve God."

Many parents want their children to believe God; the thing which usually makes us different, however, is our emphasis on serving. My goal for my children is that when they reach adulthood they will be "thoroughly furnished to every good work." To many parents, the idea of training their children to be servants is absurd, yet Jesus Himself is our example in this.

We are told in Phil. 2:5-8 that for our sake Jesus put aside His deity and took upon Himself the form of a bondservant. The attitudes which seem to us to be important in attaining the form of bondservant are these: respect for authority, praise, humility, mercy, holiness, trust, loyalty, and hospitality.

In order to infuse each attitude into the child, we define behaviors which, when required from the child repeatedly, mold his emotions into the desirable attitude. This transferring of attitudes from the parent to the child involves a process called "training."

4. *Train up a child in the way he should go, even when he is old he will not depart from it* (Prov. 22:6). There is a large difference between teaching and training. Teaching imparts knowledge; training is showing a child how to do something and then seeing that he does it. Teaching is a transfer of information in which the child is the recipient; training requires a response in which the child is the active participant.

Many parents are honestly confused about these two concepts. Frequently, I hear a distraught mother say, "I've told you over and over not to do that!" I usually have to sit on my lip to keep from saying, "Then why don't you move him so he won't do it?"

I believe Christian parents must be willing to separate themselves from the world before they can train their children to serve God. The behavior of separateness is basic to all Christian education. It is not a behavior of racism or self-righteousness. It is the realization that we are "in the world but not of the world."

Each parent who truly wants to pass on a Christian faith to his child must accept that we are a royal priesthood, a chosen generation, a people set aside from the world. "Holy (Different), Holy (Different), Holy (Different) is the Lord God of Hosts." We, too, must be different, not to gain attention nor to practice condemnation of others, but in order to remain unspotted before the Lord.

Let me say it again: one of the most important functions of a Christian parent is to provide reinforcement for being holy. We cannot teach our children to be holy if we are not willing to take a stand against evil in the world.

In many homes the battle for Christianity is lost because parents lack the intestinal fortitude (guts) to make a decision for what is true, or honorable, or right, or pure, or lovely.

Other parents drive their children away from the Lord because they are willing to call evil by its name, and to keep their children from participation in it, but they won't expend the energy to provide good alternatives.

Yet another group of parents fear the condemnation of their

children or friends for taking a stand against the popular choice, so they try not to make a decision. They have deluded themselves because in this situation a non-choice is always a vote for evil.

The reason children cannot be holy unless the parents are willing to be separate is because they lack the discernment and courage to go against the world. Even though their tender consciences are pricked at the introduction of some new evil, they soon wear down and then harden. Telling a child something is evil will not protect him from it; rather, providing him with other choices and standing beside him will save him.

Parents have many opportunities each day to train their children to be separate. Driving the speed limit is holy. Prayerfully selecting friends is holy. Providing an alternative celebration to Halloween is holy.

"Owing no man anything except love" is also holy. Credit can be one of the most enslaving evils in our society. In the last ten years we have received dozens of unsolicited credit cards. I used them, and overused them, and abused them. Finally, the Lord did a cleansing work on me and one was called back. That caused me to realize my dependence on credit. I realized the clothes I bought for summer weren't paid for when it was time to buy school clothes.

Eventually, both George and I destroyed all our personal credit cards. We have found new freedom in paying cash as we go. In addition, it has helped free us from enslavement to materialism. Before, if we saw something we wanted and our credit limit could stand it, we bought it. Frequently now, we must save to buy it or make do with what we have.

Protecting our children from the mass media is holy. If television, newspapers, and magazines were totally free of violence and pornography, I would still hesitate to use them because of the power of suggestion they have.

Even though I have consciously isolated myself from the media, it seems that when quiche is an "in" thing to be cooking, I'm cooking it. If brown and orange are the most popular fall colors, they "happen" to be my choices for fall. If *Parent Effectiveness Training* is the current rage in books for parents, I'm reading it.

The fact that I am right in step with the culture even though I am consciously trying not to be influenced by it, is really scary to me. It leaves me on my knees before the Lord, seeking the discipline to go to the grocery without being overpowered.

Satan is king over the earth, and we as Christian parents must prayerfully discern the things which are of his kingdom and refuse to participate in them. Only then can our children be holy to the Lord.

Training is the transferring of control from the parent to the child and requires the active participation of the parent. It is doing something before a child, with a child, or to a child until the child automatically chooses to do it that way. Parental control of the child gradually lessens and the child's self-control takes over.

If I want my child to practice helpfulness (an important behavior in forming an attitude of humility) then I joyfully help him. I let him help me and I receive that helpfulness with gladness. He is encouraged to help others even to the point of self-sacrifice. I also share stories from the Bible about how Jesus, or Peter, or Joseph helped, but the reason the child learns to put aside his selfishness and practice helpfulness is because he is living it.

Self-control is a behavior which can be called forth from a very small child. A parent who has his emotions in check can guide a child to successfully master his own emotions.

Frequently, a child becomes tearful as a result of anger, fear, or pain. Those are serious emotions which need to be dealt with seriously. However, many times a parent allows the original trauma to turn into hysteria, and that is very wrong for the child. Hysteria is only loud self-pity and doesn't profit anything. By dealing with the situation in a calm and reassuring manner, the parent can comfort the child and encourage him to keep his emotions in check.

There are many other ways parents can teach self-control. Often my self-control in action involves keeping my mouth shut. When Julie pours grease down the leg of her new pants, I must be quiet. Obviously, she wouldn't *choose* to mess up her new clothes. My most Christlike response is to sympathize with her dilemma and help clean it up. When someone in front of me makes a right turn from the left lane, I need to be quiet. While my condemnation of the act might be justified, my anger shows a lack of self-control.

Self-control also suggests no excesses in any area of the flesh. Too much work is excess, too much exercise is excess, too much pie is excess. We must train our children to recognize and control the difference between what our bodies need and what they want. I heard a statistic the other day which said that more than 50 percent of all Americans are overweight. That is a visible lack of self-control.

Placing children in an orderly environment is another means of helping them gain self-control. I have already confessed I am not the world's best housekeeper, but there is a definite order to our lives. A child who actively participates in establishing order in his space and within the household is more likely to believe he can control his emotions.

5. *Withhold not correction from the child . . .* Of course punishment is a necessary force in training a child; I believe it must be meted out swiftly and consistently for each case of disobedience. However, I don't like to punish my children. I get a heartache almost every time I have to correct them. The style of preventive discipline I have mentioned so often in the preceding chapters is the result of our desire not to punish the children. When disobedience does occur, the immediate need is to get the child's attention. That will require discipline—possibly the rod—in order to restrain the child's improper behavior. The next step is to involve the child in the responsibility for his own life.

Our usual form of discipline is to remove the child from the area where the conflict is taking place. A younger child who is being punished is removed from the scene and carried to his room at about the speed of light. We do not engage in any discussion about the act before he is removed. He is left in his room, on his bed, with the admonition to stay there until we come to get him.

No more than *five minutes* later, we go in and explain why the behavior was inappropriate, and what the positive choices are. The older children are dealt with in a similar manner except they are encouraged to remove themselves quickly and when we go to talk with them we let them tell us what they did wrong.

Once a child has been instructed on what is expected from him, we deal with him the *first time* he disobeys. Punishment which follows wrong behavior immediately is much more effective than delayed correction. The young child doesn't connect the restraint with the misbehavior if there is a time lag between the two.

Whenever we are initiating a new behavior pattern, we interact with the child every time he acts, not only with punishment if he is wrong, but also with reward if he is right. Once he exhibits any of the positive behavior, we reward him with attention or approval or affection. We might say, "That is just what I wanted you to do," or "It makes me feel good that you did it that way."

Once the new behavior begins to be a habit, we shift our attention to some new area of growth and only occasionally offer reinforcement. In other words, we begin to assume he has internalized the concept and doesn't need us to constantly comment on it.

The good news is that children who are nurtured in a creative, joyful home do not have to be punished very often. With our extended family, we provide so many activities for positive growth and interaction that the children are hustling all the time to do what is expected of them so they can participate in the merrymaking. They are so busy doing the do's that they don't have time to do the don'ts.

The nurturing of children is a full-time job. In Deut. 6:1–9 the writer instructs us to constantly teach our children to love God. Any mother or father who chooses to obey God by training his children night and day will not be plagued with the boredom and restlessness evident in most of our culture.

Both George and I find that each day our hearts turn more toward home as we seek to work out God's plan for our family.

15140

HQ Andrews, Sheryl J.
769
A576 Our children, our
1977   friends

DATE			
DEC -5 '94			
DE 27 '95			
AP 29 '96			
DE 04 '96			

HIEBERT LIBRARY
Pacific College - M. B. Seminary
Fresno, Calif. 93702

© THE BAKER & TAYLOR CO.